LIVING IN SCOTLAND, 1760–1820

P 51

2, 5, 8.

∧

2 breed & effect

Fig. 1. – A section from A. and M. Armstrong's map of Ayrshire, dated 1775.

LIVING IN SCOTLAND, 1760–1820

by

A. D. CAMERON

Principal Teacher of History
Inverness Royal Academy

OLIVER & BOYD

Oliver & Boyd Ltd

Tweeddale Court Edinburgh

05 002004 8

Set in Monotype 9 on 11 pt. Times
Printed in Great Britain by
Cox & Wyman Ltd,
London, Fakenham and Reading

CONTENTS

PREFACE

Intended mainly for third and fourth year pupils, this book has been written in the spirit of the Alternative Syllabus for Ordinary Grade in History. It is neither a text-book nor a source-book but something between the two – a collection of historical material which pupils can use to create for themselves a picture of what it was like to be living in Scotland at that time.

The documents have been kept as short and simple as possible, less essential parts have been omitted but care has been taken not to distort the meaning of the original.

Many people in and out of libraries have helped in finding suitable material, notably Miss Dickson of the Scottish Room, Central Public Library, Edinburgh; Mr. Lachlan Dick, my colleague in Inverness, and Mr. Alexander Fenton and Mr. Stuart Maxwell, both of the National Museum of Antiquities. Mr. John Mackay drew the maps and illustrated the Time Chart. I am very grateful to all of them.

A. D. Cameron.

Inverness,
August, 1969

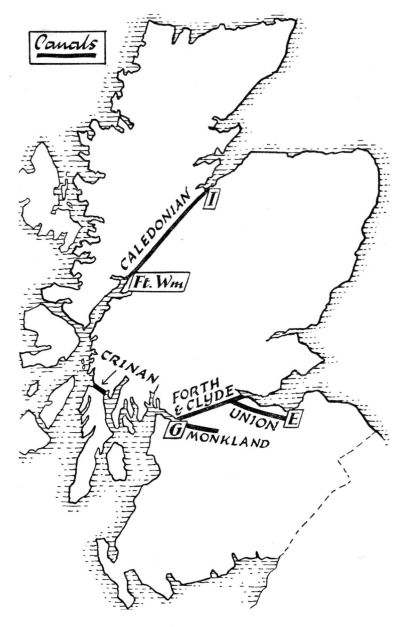

Fig. 2. – Canals in Scotland.

1·EFFECTS OF THE UNION AND THE 'FORTY-FIVE

The Union of 1707

Although at first the Scots found it difficult to compete with their more prosperous southern neighbours, increased contact with England provided new ideas, for example in agriculture and the iron industry, while access to colonial trade brought in new wealth, particularly to Glasgow:

We hae our Stirling serges, Musselburgh stuffs, Aberdeen hose, Edinburgh shalloons and the like for our woollen and worsted goods – and we hae linens of a' kinds better and cheaper than you hae in Lunnon itsel' – and we can buy your north o' England wares, as cheap as you can at Liverpool – and we are making a fair spell at cottons and muslins. Ye'll find, sir, us Glasgow folk no sae far ahint, but what we may follow.

> Bailie Nicol Jarvie in SIR WALTER SCOTT'S *Rob Roy* [Fiction]

I now took pleasure in planting, and in enclosing; but because I did not like the husbandry practised in this country I got some farmers from Dorsetshire. This made me divide my ground; I made strips of planting (woods) between every enclosure, some forty, fifty, sixty feet broad, to be a great shelter and warm the ground.

> 6TH EARL OF HADDINGTON, *A Treatise on the Manner of Raising Forest Trees*, p. 92

The first benefit which this town of Glasgow derived from the Union was the large share it took with England, in the Virginia tobacco trade. Since the American Revolution this article of commerce and manufacture has greatly declined throughout the whole kingdom; but I was informed that, in the year 1772, out of ninety thousand hogsheads of tobacco imported from Virginia to Great Britain, the town of Glasgow alone, engrossed forty-nine thousand.

> I. LETTICE, *Letters on a Tour through Scotland*, p. 82, 1794

It was after the Union that the merchants of Stornoway had full scope for their laudable pursuits: then it was, that the herrings which they caught, might lawfully be sent to the British West-India Islands, and exported thither, and to all other lawful places, attended with the encouragement of a bounty: from that time the people of Stornoway have

1

been gradually advancing. Now they can show in their harbour, in the fishing time, upward of thirty sail of stout handsome vessels, from twenty to seventy tons burden, all their own property. Their town is a pattern of neatness and cleanliness.

P. WHITE, *The Present State of the Scotch Fisheries*, p. 47, 1791

Till the Union made the Scots acquainted with English manners, the culture of their lands was unskilful, and their domestic life unformed; their tables were coarse as the feasts of Eskimoes, and their houses filthy as the cottages of Hottentots. Since then, their progress in useful knowledge has been rapid and uniform.

DR. SAMUEL JOHNSON, *Journey to the Western Islands*, p. 50, 1773

You will find it useful to deal with these short answer questions on the left-hand pages of your workbook and reserve the pages opposite them for the longer answers suggested under the heading, *To guide your writing*, which you will find at the end of each chapter. If you answer the short questions in sentences, the information you compile on the left will help in your work on the right:

1. Shalloons are closely woven woollen cloth: see if you can identify the other kinds of cloth mentioned by Bailie Nicol Jarvie.
2. Why was Bailie Nicol Jarvie optimistic about Scotland's prospects after the Union?
3. How were the Earl of Haddington's methods of farming changed by English practice?
4. In what ways did (*a*) Glasgow and (*b*) Stornoway profit from the Union?
5. (*a*) How did Dr. Johnson think the Scots had benefited from association with England?
   (*b*) What nationality do you think he was?

The Highlands after Culloden

After the defeat of Prince Charles' Jacobite army on bleak Culloden Moor in 1746, the Government forces devastated the glens with fire and sword. New laws were enacted to destroy those features of Highland life which had made that Jacobite rising possible, and military forces patrolled the Highlands to enforce them. Jacobite chiefs were in exile, and their estates were forfeited to the Crown, to be administered by Government agents. When the heritable jurisdictions, the right of chiefs to hold courts to try their clansmen, were all abolished, this law and the steps taken to disarm the Highlanders did much to destroy the authority of the chief, making him no longer a dispenser of justice, no longer a military leader.

The Act against carrying weapons and wearing Highland dress, which was typical of the new legislation, was strictly applied for ten years, although it was not repealed until 1782. People had to swear this oath:

'I, A. B., do swear as I shall answer to God at the great day of judgment, I have not, nor shall have in my possession any gun, sword, pistol or arm whatever, and never use tartan, plaid, or any part of the Highland garb; and if I do so, may I be cursed, may I never see my wife and children, father, mother or relations, and lie without Christian burial in a strange land, far from the graves of my forefathers and my kindred; may all this come across me if I break my oath.'

D. MITCHELL, *History of the Highlands and Gaelic Scotland*, p. 663

The reports of officers in the Highlands to the Commander-in-Chief, Scotland, in 1752 reveal the activities of Government forces:

The patrolling party surprised and took one Donald M'Donald. He had a large French musket, loaded with large shot and slugs. I tried to find out whose gun it was but could make nothing of him. I sent him to Inverness with two men. He has since been tried before the sheriff and sentenced to undergo the penalty of the law.

Capt. A. Trapaud.

The corporal at Glen Strathfarrar took up one Hugh Fraser for wearing the philabeg [kilt]. As they crossed the Dejag, which was scarce fordable, the prisoner let drop his philabeg in the river under cover of his great coat. I sent him prisoner to the sheriff-substitute at Inverness and after examination he was set at liberty.

Capt. A. Trapaud.

Seeing some people armed, driving cattle on the north side of Loch Lyon, I examined them and found them to be dealers in cattle from Breadalbane. Their names were M'Nab and M'Intyre. They had passes and protections from Lord Breadalbane for carrying arms.

Lieut. Alex. Tennant.

Captain Campbell of Glen Lyon came here to Loch Rannoch and showed me two warrants from the Sheriff-Depute of Perthshire, for arresting Charles Stewart, an attainted rebel, and Allan Breck Stewart, the supposed murderer of Mr. Campbell of Glenure. I gave the description of the two persons to my patrolling parties, with orders to apprehend them.

Capt. Walter Johnstone.

R. REID, *Glasgow Past and Present*, vol. 3, Appendix pp. 795–810, 1856

I am much of your opinion, that, without a considerable aid of foreign troops, the Highlanders will never stir. The spirit of revenge is prevalent amongst them but the risk is too great without help; however we ought to be cautious and vigilant. We ought to have a good store of meal in the forts, plenty of entrenching tools, and a few well-chosen posts in the middle of those clans most likely to rebel, with a force sufficient to entrench and defend themselves, and with positive orders never to surrender.

> Letter to Captain Rickson at Inverness from James Wolfe in 1755. Wolfe had fought at Culloden and was to die victorious in the battle of Quebec against the French in 1759. R. REID, *Glasgow Past and Present*, vol. 3, p. 783, 1856

1. What seems to have been the punishment for owning weapons or wearing Highland dress?
2. (*a*) Why was Donald M'Donald sentenced?
   (*b*) Why was Hugh Fraser set free?
   (*c*) Why were M'Nab and M'Intyre not arrested?
3. Look up R. L. Stevenson's novel, *Kidnapped*, for an exciting account of the murder of Campbell of Glenure.
4. What was James Wolfe's opinion of the chances of another Jacobite rising in 1755?

Britain in 1760

There was not any period when the temper and spirit of the British nation were more in unison than in the later years of George II. The general gloom and despondency diffused by the disgraceful events which happened at the commencement of the war with France [1756] were not only dispelled by the vigorous administration of Mr. [William, later known as the Elder] Pitt, and by a series of the most brilliant exploits in the annals of Britain, but gave place to pride and exultation. These feelings were heightened by the accession of our present gracious sovereign, George III. The circumstances of his being a native of Britain, his excellent character, and the retrieved glory of the nation, all combined to bring forth the loyalty of all descriptions of men. Even the Jacobites renounced their opposition to the house of Hanover, and wished to be acknowledged as good subjects.

> DR. THOMAS SOMERVILLE, *My Own Life and Times*, pp. 51-2

1. What reasons does Somerville give for these feelings of unity and pride on the part of the British nation?
2. How have the Jacobites changed?

To guide your writing

1. What were the general effects of the Union on Scottish trade and agriculture?
2. As a Highlander, write your reactions to the Government's treatment of your people after Culloden.
3. What would probably be the attitude of Lowland or English M.P.s to Government policy in the Highlands?
4. What evidence is there for the view that the danger from Jacobitism was over by 1760?

2·WORK IN THE COUNTRY

Farming before the Improvers

It was not until the eighteenth century that the system of land-holding and methods of farming began to change in Scotland. Previously, each group of tenants lived in a small cluster of houses, called a *toun* and farmed on the surrounding land. They produced their own food and clothing and they sold any surplus they had in a nearby market. They had to pay rent either in money or in produce and were often expected to perform certain labour services as well, in return for the use of the land:

The Use of Land

RUNRIG: The lands around the village, after being laid off into fields of various extent and quality, called *infield*, were subdivided into as many parcels as ridges as corresponded to the number of retainers, in equal portions, each having *rig and rig about*, or alternately through all the fields, so that everyone might have an equal share. From this mode of occupation, this was called *runrig* possession.

GEORGE ROBERTSON, *Rural Recollections*, 1829

INFIELD AND OUTFIELD: Fifty years ago, the land was always occupied in runrig by the different tenants. The land was divided into outfield and infield. The land near the farm-houses, called infield, was cropped alternately with oats and barley. The whole dung was laid upon the barley crop; in some cases the farmers unroofed their houses and dug turf from the best spots of their natural grass-fields to increase the quality of their dung. (Parts of the outfield were cultivated from time to time but most of it was used for pasture.)

G. ROBERTSON, *General View of the Agriculture of the County of Perth*, 1799

Difficulties in Farming

THE RIGS: Each farmer's cultivated strips sloped inwards and upwards sometimes to a height of 3 feet:

To prevent any of the soil being carried to the adjoining ridge, each individual makes his own ridge as high as possible.

SIR JOHN SINCLAIR, *Husbandry of Scotland*, 1814

THE PLOUGH: The plough was pulled by a team of six or eight oxen, provided by the tenants jointly:

The Scots plough is a strong, heavy machine about thirteen feet in length overall. When well made it is very proper for breaking up or tilling rough uncultivated grounds; its weight prevents it being easily thrown out by stones. In tender soils it is not so profitable for, by its great weight, the friction is increased, on account of which more power must be required to draw it than what is necessary with a lighter and better plough.

General Report of the Agriculture of Scotland, 1814

LACK OF WINTER FODDER: Many cattle and sheep died in winter because of the shortage of grass and hay:

Even in late April, the country at large lay a mere waste; nothing to be seen but stones and dry blades of couch grass; the pasture and meadow lands gnawed to the quick, and strewed with the dead carcases of sheep.

MARSHALL, *General View of the Agriculture of the Central Highlands*, 1794

The burdens on small farmers

RENT: One of the small village farms by-and-by becoming vacant, my mother advised the taking of fourteen acres for as many pounds of yearly rent . . . They kept a cow, sometimes two, and a pet sheep (and *Pet Nanny* was little behind a Highland cow, quality and quantity of the milk considered). The best of my father's years were exhausted in draining, ploughing and tugging through the day and shoemaking half the night. However, being of an excellent constitution, he wore well!

JOHN YOUNGER, Shoemaker, *Autobiography*, p. 14

OBLIGATIONS: The farmers having no leases, or short ones, were extremely poor. They were also bound to grind their corn at the mill of the barony (this obligation was known as *thirlage*) and to employ the proprietor's blacksmith. They paid double price for their work at the mill and the blacksmith's shop and were besides saucily and ill served. The proprietor received a rent on this account from the miller and the blacksmith.

G. DEMPSTER, *State of the Northern Parts of Scotland*, quoted in *Letters to Sir Adam Fergusson*, ed. SIR JAMES FERGUSSON, p. 48

Part of the dues to the miller were for the upkeep of the mill, arising out of thirlage, and the other part, called *multures*, was the fee for grinding corn and could amount to one-tenth of its value.

PERSONAL SERVICES: In the summer, the only Season for Improvement, I am toiling, casting, winning and leading leet Peats out of a worn out Moss (to pay part of his rent in kind to the Laird): my servants and I are compelled to labour six days picking Straws and Stones out of the Highway; we are as many days making Hay for the Laird, shearing and leading his Corn; I must plough too and harrow, both for him and the Minister; my Men and my Horses are every now and then trotting to Aberdeen as Carriers, as often as I am warned by his Officer. And when I am at Liberty, I must be repairing my Houses, which (need) perpetual mending, and which I am bound to leave in good Condition; I am often forced to lead Lime and Slates from a great way off, not only for the Laird, but for his neighbours, at his desire; and when the Kirk or the Manse need repairs, I never want work at one or other of these Works all Summer over.

> Tenant's letter to *Aberdeen Journal* (1750), quoted by
> H. HAMILTON, *Economic History of Scotland in the Eighteenth Century*, p. 52

1. Explain the following terms: runrig; thirlage; multures.
2. What use was made of (*a*) infield and (*b*) outfield?
3. Why were rigs high in the centre?
4. How much rent did John Younger's father pay per acre?
5. Make a list of the duties the tenant who wrote the letter had to perform (*a*) for his landlord and (*b*) for the minister.
6. What does he mean by his statement, 'I never want work . . . all Summer over'?

To guide your writing.
1. As a small farmer living then, explain the burdens and difficulties of your occupation.
2. As a landowner who is prepared to make changes, point out the ways in which you think this system of farming is inefficient.

The Improvement of Farming and its Effects

One of the effects of the Union of 1707 was that more Scots travelled in England. Scottish landowners in particular were impressed by the best methods of agriculture they saw there and returned determined to improve their own estates and make them more productive. Two acts of 1695, passed by the old Scottish parliament, proved useful to landlords because they permitted them to make compact farms out of lands lying runrig and to divide wasteland or pasture among them, without worrying about tenants' rights:

Enclosure of Common Land in England

There are but two modes of enclosure of commons. First by unanimous consent of the parties claiming rights. Secondly by Act of Parliament obtained by the petition of a certain proportion of the commoners, both in number and in value.

In point of economy, the first of these methods is most eligible, as it saves the expense of an Act of Parliament but it is seldom accomplished from the difficulty of procuring the consent of every individual tenant.

Survey of the Board of Agriculture for Somersetshire, 1798

1. (*a*) Why was the first method in England thought preferable to the second?
   (*b*) Why then was it so seldom adopted?
2. In which country did the landlords have greater power?

Improvements in Land Use and Farming Methods in Scotland

The following extracts show how far these had gone by the 1790's:

A large tract of land, called Mauchlin-muir, has, of late years, been turned into arable land and properly enclosed and surrounded with belts of trees, by the late Sir Thomas Miller.

The Statistical Account of Scotland,* vol. 2, p. 110, Mauchlin, Ayrshire

The two greatest heritors have each taken a great quantity of land into their own possession in order to enclose and improve it by draining, planting, etc.

O.S.A., vol. 10, p. 242, Cluny, Aberdeenshire

The ploughing is now most frequently carried on by two horses and James Small's plough has been introduced. A great many of the old farmers regret the passing of the old Scots plough and affirm that their soil requires a deep and large furrow.

O.S.A., vol. 18, p. 192, West Calder, Midlothian

Wheat, oats, barley, turnips, potatoes are here cultivated with a success which even the richest counties of England might envy. The subdivision and enclosure of the fields; the rotation of crops, adopted for the purpose of continually enjoying, yet without exhausting the fertility of the soil; the choice of seeds; the culture of the ground by tillage, manuring, weeding, watering; and the opulence which many of the

---

* *The Statistical Account of Scotland* ed. by Sir John Sinclair and published by William Creech in the 1790's is today popularly designated *The Old* to distinguish it from *The New* which came out fifty years later. It will be referred to here as O.S.A.

B

farmers have acquired by the fair use of their industry and capital, distinguish the shire of Berwick as a district in which agriculture has been happily carried to high perfection.

R. HERON, *Topographical Description of Scotland*, p. 28, 1797

It appears from the face of the country, from those rough grounds and moorlands, which within a few years, have been converted into beautiful and fertile cornfields, that modern husbandry is well understood by the farmers. Flax and potatoes are raised in considerable quantities. Cabbage and turnip also are grown for feeding cattle and raising young stock.

O.S.A., vol 18, pp. 73–4, Scone, Perthshire

1. What sort of people took the lead in enclosing land and improving farming?
2. What new crops are mentioned above, compared with under the runrig system?
3. What is the meaning of: arable; enclosed; heritor; opulence?
4. What is the purpose of a rotation of crops?
5. Was farming in Berwickshire typical or exceptional in Scotland in 1797?

How some people suffered

There is considerable evidence to show that some poor tenants suffered from the changes in farming:

Warning to nineteen tenants in several farms and four occupiers of houses in the Kirktoun: to flitt and remove themselves, their wives, bairns, family, servants, cottars, dependents, goods and gear from their respective tacks, houses and possessions at the Term of Whitsunday next to come.

Monymusk Papers, quoted in H. HAMILTON, *Economic History of Scotland in the Eighteenth Century*, p. 83

After [my father was ejected] and four or five of these small farms had been thrown into one the whole was let to one of their own number.

Still amongst their own customers, with some small debts still due to them about the place, they [my parents] felt inclined to linger in the village; and, as the house they occupied was then to let singly, they took it still for the coming year and became simply cottars, retaining nothing of their former stock but three or four barn-door hens.

JOHN YOUNGER, Shoemaker, *Autobiography*, pp. 57–8

Its present occupant has within a few years managed to dispossess seven or eight dependent cottagers, who from father to son had maintained themselves comfortably, brought up their children with decency and given them a useful education. These, being turned adrift found no other resource at least for their children, than that of sending them to the great manufactories.

Elvanfoot, Clydesdale.

I. LETTICE, *Letters on a Tour through Scotland in 1792*

1. In all three extracts, what did the tenants lose?
2. In what way did the Younger family suffer less than the tenants at Monymusk?
3. What were 'great manufactories'?
4. What seems to have happened to the size of farms?

How some people benefited

SMALL TENANTS: I have already thirty new settlers all busily employed whitening our moors, as we call converting them into arable land without expense to the proprietor – but also without profit, for they pay only a rent of 1s a year the first generation, but the full value every succeeding one. You would wonder at the change the little tenants have made on their houses and farms here since they know they are not to be removed and are rid of services. Their houses are now mostly of stone and whitened, shining like a Negro's teeth through the black muirs.

GEORGE DEMPSTER, *Letters to Sir Adam Fergusson,*
pp. 251–2, 1794

RISING FARMERS: But now the [farmers'] wives, hitherto as plain as a barn door, under first low-taken leases and war-rising markets, began to look up to and imitate the style of small gentry. The tenant or his son began to ride a mad blood horse to market; probably dined at the Club; likely became a Yeomanry-Cavalry man, bold and terrible. Hence as they afield became mighty, the mistress at home grew quite madamish; while a pianoforte and other *et ceteras* must be had for Miss the daughter.

JOHN YOUNGER, Shoemaker, *Autobiography*, p. 171

FARM WORKERS: For the evidence of higher wages being paid to farm servants see the chapter on Standards of Living, Workers in the Country.

LANDLORDS: Proof that rents were raised is given in the same chapter. Improving landlords obviously invested a great deal of money improving their land. In some cases, they rashly spent too much, but most of them gained more than they spent. Their stately country houses bear witness to this. They were fortunate that the demand for food from home resources increased as population grew and Britain waged war against revolutionary France. An extreme example of the rapid rise in the value of an estate is quoted here from H. Hamilton's *Economic History of Scotland in the Eighteenth Century*, p. 86:

In East Lothian on an estate of 626 Scots acres, the free rent in 1779 was £739 and the price of the estate £18,472; after an expenditure of little more than £2,000 on enclosing and improvements, the rent was increased to £1,300 and in 1798 the estate was sold for £57,000, three times the sum paid in 1779.

1. Why did George Dempster's tenants work so hard?
2. What is meant by: rid of services; leases; war-rising markets; gentry; rent?

To guide your writing.
1. As if you were a landlord in the eighteenth century, explain (*a*) your plans to improve your estate and (*b*) why you want to do so.
2. As a landlord, explain the benefits to the whole country caused by Improvers like yourself.
3. What features of the landscape today are the result of changes made by the Improvers? (See Fig. 1 the map of Ayrshire).
4. Why did some country folk welcome and others condemn the changes in agriculture between 1760 and 1820?
5. Do you think Dempster's plan to create more small farms was wiser than the practice of other landlords who were making larger, but fewer, farms? Give reasons for your answer.
6. The *Old Statistical Account of Scotland*, is an excellent source of information about these changes in agriculture. In every parish in Scotland, the local minister was asked to write an account of the history, life and work of the people. Some are full of facts and figures while others are written differently, like the one for Lochcarron in Ross-shire which includes these lines:

Now good Sir John it was for you
I gathered all my news
But you will say that I forgot
To count the sheep and cows

Of these we have a number too
(But then twixt you and I)
The number they would never tell
For fear the beasts would die.

REV. LACHLAN MACKENZIE.
O.S.A., vol. 13, pp. 560–1, Lochcarron

You should be able to find it in your public library. Use it
  (a) to find (i) the state of farming in your parish then,
                (ii) how much land had been enclosed,
       and (iii) the effects of the changes on the people.
  (b) to compare the situation in your parish with other parishes
       in your own county, and
  (c) to compare parishes in different areas of Scotland, e.g. one in
       the Highlands, one in the Lothians, one in Ayrshire, one in
       Galloway, and one in the Borders, to try to find out (i) what
       kind of farming was practised in each and (ii) which area was
       farthest ahead in agricultural improvement.

Other very useful sources are the reports called the 'General View of
the Agriculture of the County of ——,' one for each county in 1793–5,
and again for most counties between 1809 and 1816.

The Cattle Trade from the Highlands

Since the land in the Highlands was mostly suitable for pasture rather
than cultivation, cattle were bred and, when sold in southern markets,
proved to be the Highlanders' main source of money:

Black Cattle

The most profitable breed of cattle, and that which is found best suited
for Argyllshire is the true West Highland breed. The form most wished
for is to get them short in the legs, round in the body, straight in the back
and long in the snout. They are of various colours, black, dun, branded
and brown; but the black is the most common, and the most run upon.

When in good condition and from three to four years old, when they
are commonly sold off, the carcase may weigh 360 to 400 lb. But such as
are brought to better pasture as in England, may be brought to weigh
560 lb. or more.

J. SMITH, *General View of the Agriculture of the County
of Argyll*, p. 235, 1798

Pitmain Tryst, a Highland cattle market

A tryst is a pre-arranged meeting for buyers and sellers of cattle:

Then came the Pitmain Tryst. It was an old custom to hold a cattle
market yearly in the month of September on a moor between Kingussie
and Pitmain. The Highland proprietors reared large stocks of young

cattle. (Macpherson of) Belleville had every year a hundred stots (young bullocks), sold generally for from £7 to £8 apiece. Though great pains were taken to improve my father's stock, Belleville generally got the top price at the Tryst. The buyers were drovers who bought, and paid for, and carried off their purchase in large herds to the south, either to be privately disposed of or resold at Falkirk for the English market.

After the market in the morning, there was a dinner in the evening, drovers, farmers and lairds all meeting in a large room at Pitmain to enjoy the best cheer the county afforded. Lord Huntly presided and sent a stag from Gaick forest. Very grand speeches my father and others made after the punch began to circulate!

ELIZABETH GRANT OF ROTHIEMURCHUS, *Memoirs of a Highland Lady*, pp. 273–4, 1911. Ed. LADY STRACHEY

1. How often was Pitmain Tryst held?
2. Who bought cattle there?
3. Where were the cattle taken?
4. What were the main ingredients of 'the best cheer'?

The Drovers

The Highlanders are masters of the difficult trade of driving [or droving] which seems to suit them as well as the trade of war. They know perfectly the drove roads which lie over the wildest tracks of the country, and avoid as much as possible the highways, which distress the feet of the bullocks, and the turnpikes which annoy the spirit of the drovers; whereas, on the broad green or grey track across the moor, the herd not only moves at ease but may pick up a mouthful of food by the way. At night, the drovers usually sleep along with their cattle, let the weather be what it will; and many of these hardy men do not rest under a roof during the journey from Lochaber to Lincolnshire. They are paid very highly, for it depends on their prudence, vigilance and honesty, whether the cattle reach the final market in good order.

The Highland drover carried a few handfuls of oatmeal and two or three onions, renewed from time to time, and a ram's horn of whisky, which he used regularly but sparingly, every night and morning. His dirk, so worn as to be concealed beneath the arm or the folds of his plaid was his only weapon, excepting the cudgel with which he directed the movements of the cattle.

A Highlander was never so happy as on these occasions. There was a variety in the whole journey; there were the constant change of place and scene and the intercourse with the various farmers, graziers and traders, intermingled with occasional merry-makings; and there was the consciousness of superior skill. The Highlander, a child amongst flocks, is a prince amongst herds, and disdaining the shepherd's slothful life, he

feels himself nowhere more at home than when following a gallant drove
of his cattle in the character of their guardian.

SIR WALTER SCOTT, *The Two Drovers* [Fiction].
Waverley Novels, vol. xli (A. & C. Black), pp. 310–14

1. What is a drove road?
2. What were turnpikes and why did the drovers wish to avoid them?
   (See the section on Roads on page 51.)
3. What qualities did a good drover need?
4. 'In the character of their guardian' – against what dangers do you
   think the drovers would have to guard?

Falkirk Tryst

Falkirk trysts were originally held upon a large common in the vicinity
of Falkirk: they are now held upon a field in the parish of Larbert, but
though the site be changed, the original name remains.

The first Falkirk tryst is generally held upon the second Tuesday of
August. There are generally exhibited 5 to 6,000 cattle.

The second tryst is held on the second Tuesday of September. There are
generally exhibited 15,000 black cattle and 15,000 sheep.

The third tryst is held upon the second Tuesday of October, when there
are generally exhibited from 25,000–30,000 black cattle, even 40,000 have
been known at this tryst; there are also, at an average, 25,000 sheep
exposed for sale.

At the last two trysts, especially at that of October, a great number of
horses are also exposed for sale.

Thus it appears that there are annually exhibited at these trysts above
50,000 black cattle and 40,000 sheep. Taking the former at an average
value of £8 (compared with £4 in 1792) and the latter at 15s each, the
value of the whole will amount to £430,000.

P. GRAHAM, *General View of the
Agriculture of Stirlingshire*, 1812

As they plodded along the road they encountered many other droves
till it was like a river of cattle rolling towards Stenhousemuir. The air
was noisy with the shouts of the drovers, the whacks of their sticks, the
barking of their dogs and the lowing of the cattle. It was hard hot work
running hither and thither to keep the herd together.

[Here at the Falkirk Tryst] the drovers stood with their cattle in the
centre, all trying to keep their herds separate from each other. Around
the field tents and booths were set up and over open fires huge cauldrons
of meat-broth simmered, that the drovers were buying at threepence
the bowl. In the tents men were selling whisky and ale.

Among the herds, the English and Lowland buyers wandered, poking this beast and feeling the sides of that one. So many different voices – the soft slow speech of the Highlander, the gruff Yorkshire dialect, the burr of the Cumberland tongue, the sharper Cockney voices of the men from the London markets. Over all these tongues was the babel of hucksters calling their wares, the sound of music played on a fiddle competing with the drone of the bagpipes, the barking of dogs, the shouts of the drovers, the plaintive cries of the sheep and the constant lowing of the cattle.

KATHLEEN FIDLER, *The Drover Lad* [Fiction], pp. 79-80

1. How many times a year was a tryst held at Falkirk?
2. How many cattle were sold annually at Falkirk, the biggest cattle market in Scotland?
3. Find out what was happening between 1792 and 1812 which caused the price of cattle to be doubled.
4. Where did the buyers come from?

The Value of the Cattle Trade

The value of the animals which changed hands at Falkirk is given above in Graham's account in 1812. The benefits this trade brought to some individuals in the Highlands and to the country in general are evident from the next two writers:

Mackinnon of Coirechatachan [in Skye] pays about £50 in rent. But by droving and selling meal, in the former part of his life, he has made as much money as that the interest of it will pay his rent.

JAMES BOSWELL, *Tour to the Hebrides*, p. 125

Had the Scotch cattle been always confined to the market of Scotland, in a country in which the quantity of land which can be applied to no other purpose but the feeding of cattle is so great, it is scarce possible that their price could ever have risen so high as to render it profitable to cultivate land for the sake of feeding them. In England, the price of cattle seems, in the neighbourhood of London, to have got to this height at the beginning of the last century. Of all the commercial advantages which Scotland has derived from the Union with England, this rise in the price of cattle is, perhaps, the greatest. It has not only raised the value of all Highland estates, but it has, perhaps, been the principal cause of the improvement of the low country.

ADAM SMITH, *The Wealth of Nations*
(Everyman's, Vol. 1, pp. 201–2)

1. Where is 'the low country'?
2. What does Smith consider to have been Scotland's main commercial gain from the Union with England?

To guide your writing.

1. If you live in the Highlands or Galloway, find out about cattle markets, drove roads and river fords there and trace the route followed by drovers taking cattle from there to Falkirk Tryst or on their way to England. A. R. B. Haldane's book *The Drove Roads of Scotland* contains an excellent map.

2. To compare with the figures given in the extracts, try to find out the prices paid for cattle and sheep and the carcase weight of cattle sold at auction markets today.

3. Study Kathleen Fidler's description of Falkirk Tryst and write descriptions of:

    (*a*) the drover's departure for the south,

    (*b*) a day in the life of a drover,

    (*c*) a cattle drove passing southwards through Yorkshire, as seen by a local man.

4. Using what you have learned, write an essay on the cattle trade and its value to Scotland.

3 · CHANGES IN INDUSTRY

Linen

Domestic Industry

Making cloth is an ancient craft. In their spare time at home in Scotland in the eighteenth century women and girls continued to spin yarn, which was woven into cloth on a hand-loom, either by the man of the household or by a village weaver. This domestic industry was a valuable source of income, and in many cases, such as the day labourer's family at Caputh, on p. 39, it was essential to help the family to make ends meet. John Younger recalls the importance of this activity in the Borders:

Down to . . . about the end of the French war, when steam-loom power and machinery came into general use, spinning lint yarn on the small wheel and woollen yarn on the large wheel . . . engaged every country woman's earnest occupation early and late. Throughout my mother's married life she was accustomed to rise very early, by five or six o'clock, even in cold winter mornings, for the purpose of spinning yarn to provide clothes for the family use. The *boom* of her large, and the *birr* of her small, wheel were music to my young ear on awakening in the mornings. Handloom weaving was then a thriving occupation for men throughout country villages.

One chief family duty was the growing of lint and the provision of wool. The country housewife [had] to card, spin, boil, bleach and get up a provision of necessary bed clothes for the daughters of the family (enough to furnish each two beds was considered the necessary quantity), which was called such a one's 'providing'.

JOHN YOUNGER, Shoemaker, *Autobiography*, pp. 8, 248

In other parts of Scotland, it was just as common, for example:

Many of the people manufacture their own blankets, and nearly their whole attire both of wool and of flax by their own domestic industry.
General View of the Agriculture of Moray and Nairn, 1811, p. 399

1. Name the two fibres in common use for making cloth at this time.
2. What kind of wheel was used for spinning each of them in John Younger's home?

18

3. What do you understand by: domestic industry; hand-loom; one's 'providing'?

Linen Manufacture

The manufacture of linen was the main branch of the textile industry for the first three-quarters of the eighteenth century. It gained much from Government support, especially after the appointment of the Board of Commissioners for Manufactures in 1727. Government support began before the Union, when laws were passed to encourage both the weaving and use of linen, even going as far as insisting on burying the dead in Scots linen by an Act of 1686:

'Our Soveraigne Lord, for the encouradgement of linen manufactories within this Kingdome and prevention of the exportation of the moneys thereof, for the buying and importing of linen, Doeth Statute and Ordaine That hereafter no Corps of any Person whatsoever shall be buried in any shirt, sheet or any thing else except in plaine linen made and spun within the Kingdome.'

A.P.S., viii, 598, c. 28

The Board of Commissioners, with over £2,500 a year to spend on the linen industry, was able to help it in three main ways: by building lint mills in different parts of the country where flax was prepared for spinning; by encouraging foreign experts to settle in Scotland and teach the different techniques; and by founding spinning schools to teach spinning and improve the quality of the yarn produced. These policies proved successful. By 1760 this basically hand industry was producing enough to serve the country's needs in cloth and thread, and to export some to England and the colonies.

Spinning schools and small spinning wheels were introduced to the Highlands too:

The smaller spinning wheel, adapted for flax, never obtained a footing in the Highlands till the country was disarmed. The good women used to speak most pathetically of the '46 as the sad era which introduced little wheels and red soldiers into the country.

MRS. GRANT OF LAGGAN, *Essays on the Superstitions of the Highlanders of Scotland*, vol. II, pp. 123–4

The expansion of the linen industry in Angus and Fife is evident from the *Old Statistical Account*:

Before the year 1750 there were upwards of 140 looms going in Forfar, and at present there are between 400 and 500. When trade is good (and it has been for some time past) the profits of it with the Government bounty, are sufficient to support the sober and industrious weaver against the influence of a falling market. Manufacturers are just now giving from 15s to 20s for working a piece of ten dozen yards, which a good workman will accomplish in as many days.

O.S.A., vol. 6, p. 514, Forfar

Every householder almost is a manufacturer of brown linen. Exclusive of considerable quantities of home-grown flax, the manufacturers use yearly of foreign flax, from Riga and St. Petersburg, several tons, amounting in value to more than £800. The manufacturers are in number 100.

O.S.A., vol 4, p. 238, Barrie, Angus

The kinds of linen manufactured here are bed-ticks, chequered and striped linens, with a mixture of cotton in some of them, and a low-priced species of plain linen. At present the manufacturers of Kirkcaldy employ about 810 looms. After the flax is hackled in the lint mill, the manufacturer sends it to undertakers in different parts of the country, who give it out to be spun by hand, and receive a certain commission on the quantity of yarn returned by them. Of the yarn used in making checks and ticks, about three-fourths are whitened and the remaining fourth dyed.

O.S.A., vol. 18, pp. 27–31, Kirkcaldy

Output of linen for sale increased from 2 million yards in 1728 to 11¾ million in 1760, and to 21 million in 1792. The coarse linen trade of Angus and Fife flourished in spite of the introduction of cotton but the effect of this new fibre on the fine linen trade in the west is a different story.

1. In what ways did the Board of Commissioners help the linen industry?

2. What is meant by: little wheels; red soldiers; Government bounty; lint mill; checks?

3. Where was flax imported from?

To guide your writing.

1. What evidence is there from the *Old Statistical Account* to prove that linen manufacture was prosperous in Angus in the 1790's?

2. Trace the growth of the east coast linen industry in the second half of the eighteenth century.

The Coming of Cotton

When cotton spinning was introduced to the west of Scotland in the 1770's and '80's it came suddenly with the building of great factories to house its water-driven machinery. Penicuik in Midlothian can rightly claim to have had the first cotton mill in 1778, followed by Rothesay in the next year but large-scale production of cotton yarn, using Richard Arkwright's water frame, began in 1786 in David Dale's factory village of New Lanark, below the Falls of Clyde. Dale was a linen merchant in Glasgow who gave out yarn to local weavers to make into cloth for him. He could see the prospects for cotton in an area like the west of Scotland with its skilled weavers. Soon he was involved in other spinning mills, such as Blantyre in Lanarkshire, Catrine in Ayrshire and as far away as Spinningdale in Sutherland. By 1792 New Lanark had two thousand inhabitants and by 1808 it was a tourist attraction:

Mr. David Dale of this place in the course of six years has raised a village on the banks of the Clyde, containing 2,000 persons, and erected five cotton mills, each of which contains 6,000 spindles.

Annual Register, 1792, *Chronicle*, p. 33

NEW LANARK VILLAGE and COTTON MILLS were erected by the late David Dale Esq., who, sometime before his death sold them to a company under the firm of *The Lanark and Chorlton Twist Company* of which Mr. Dale's son-in-law, Mr. Robert Owen is acting partner. To enjoy the pleasure of this grand scene, on leaving Lanark town take the pathway and at the distance of about a mile you arrive at the brink of the hill, when the village of New Lanark and Cotton Mills burst upon the view of the astonished beholder, lying in the deep valley beneath. The village consists of two broad and regular streets, about ½ mile in length, with good houses, five stories high, for the workers' families. The Cotton Mills lie in the centre of the village, and from their length, height and number of windows, present a pleasant object to the eye. There is also an elegant mansion for the manager's residence. Keeping the banks of the Clyde, cross a subterraneous aqueduct, scooped out of the rock for some hundred yards, through which the water necessary to give motion to the vast mass of machinery is conveyed from the river.

JAMES DUNCAN, *The Scotch Itinerary*, 1808, Appendix B

Other places in the west saw a similar influx of population and industry:

The number of inhabitants of the parish has been doubled in four years because of a cotton mill erected upon the Clyde.

O.S.A., vol. 2, p. 217, Blantyre

A very populous village named Pollockshaws lies in a fine valley. On the one side it is skirted with neat bleachfields, on the other with well-cultivated enclosures, and gives a delightful prospect of a manufacturing yet rural village.

The manufactures are chiefly the weaving of muslins, bleaching, printing of calicoes, and cotton-spinning. In weaving there are employed about 470 looms. There are two spinning mills, employing over 600 persons of different ages.

O.S.A., vol. 18, pp. 199, 205, Eastwood

The dyeing of Turkey red on cotton was established in Glasgow earlier than in any part of Great Britain. In the year 1785, Mr. George Mackintosh being in London, fell in with Monsieur Papillon, a Turkey red dyer from Rouen, carried him with him to Glasgow, and in conjunction with Mr. David Dale, built an extensive dye-house at Dalmarnock in this parish upon the banks of the Clyde, where cotton is dyed a real Turkey red, equal in beauty and solidity to East India colours.

O.S.A., vol. 12, p. 114, Glasgow

1. What kind of machines were used at New Lanark?
2. What provided the power to drive them?
3. What else did David Dale have built at New Lanark besides factories?
4. List the processes in cotton manufacture which are mentioned in the extracts from the *Old Statistical Account*.

Effects of the Coming of Cotton

ON DOMESTIC INDUSTRY: Spinning at home has almost wholly disappeared. Thus the old are cut off from the employment, within the power of age and suited to its disposition of 'drawing out a thread wi' little din', which used to keep time from being a burden, and to supply with the necessaries of life.

New Statistical Account of Scotland, vol. 1, p. 125, Colinton, 1839

Formerly almost all the weavers manufactured linen only, and either employed themselves, or derived their employment from others on the spot. Now they get employment from the great manufacturers in Glasgow etc. and cotton yarn is the principal material. Young women who were formerly put to the spinning wheel, now learn to flower muslin [i.e. to embroider].

O.S.A., vol. 2, p. 199, Hamilton

ON WORKERS IN COTTON FACTORIES: How they were affected is a matter of debate (see also the section on Workers in Industry on page 43). Here are two conflicting opinions written by ministers at the time:

Employment at cotton mills has, in general, been accounted injurious to health; and yet, out of a great number employed at work within the mill, only two have died since it was erected four years ago. Great care is taken to keep both the house [i.e. the factory] and machinery as clean as possible, and fresh air is carefully thrown in.

O.S.A., vol. 2, p. 217, Blantyre

The rapid increase of manufactures is neither friendly to the health nor morals of the people. In cotton mills a multitude of children spend a considerable part of their life there and are often exposed not to the best example. It is to be feared that a total ignorance of Christianity may become prevalent. The children in these works, confined, as it were to the very point of a spindle, must of course have narrow and contracted minds. While the work is going on, the finer parts of the cotton, flying off by friction, fill the atmosphere in which they breathe, with unwholesome particles, and it is probably from this cause that their appearance is so pale and sickly.

O.S.A., vol. 2, pp. 162–4, Nielston

ON SALES OF LINEN CLOTH: What has excited most general attention is the manufacturing of cotton cloths of various kinds. For this purpose cotton mills, bleachfields and print fields have been erected on almost all the streams in the neighbourhood affording water sufficient to move the machinery. The demand for cotton goods has much diminished the consumption of linen articles.

O.S.A., vol. 5, pp. 501–3, Glasgow

Linen producers were naturally worried by competition from cotton and efforts were made, for example in Dundee, to use machinery to spin flax but with little success until the 1820's.

Cotton yarn is cheaper than linen yarn: and cotton goods are very much used in place of cambrics, lawns and other expensive fabrics of flax; and they have almost totally superseded the silks. Women of all ranks from the highest to the lowest are clothed in British manufactures of cotton, from the cap on the crown of the head to the cotton stocking under the sole of the foot. With the gentlemen cotton stuffs for waistcoats have almost superseded woollen cloths, and silk stuffs, I believe, entirely; and they have the advantage, like the ladies' gowns, of having a new and fresh appearance every time they are washed.

DAVID MACPHERSON, *Annals of Commerce*, vol. IV, p. 81

1. What were the effects of the cotton industry on (*a*) hand spinners and (*b*) linen weavers?
2. (*a*) Which report suggests that workers' health suffered from factory work and (*b*) which does not?
   (*c*) Who was one of the employers associated with the latter place?
3. What are: cambrics; lawns?
4. Why did cotton prove more popular than linen for articles of clothing?
5. In spite of the two passages under the heading, On sales of linen cloth, the output figures for linen in Scotland, given at the end of the section on the linen industry, show a considerable rise between 1760 and 1792. Which branch of the linen industry was it that suffered from competition from cotton?

To guide your writing.
1. Why did the building of New Lanark excite so much public interest?
2. Show how the linen trade in the west was affected by the rise of the cotton industry.
3. How did people's clothing change as a result of the Industrial Revolution in textiles? For further information see *Scottish Costume 1550–1850* by Stuart Maxwell and Robin Hutchinson (A. & C. Black).

The Woollen Industry

In contrast to the manufacture of linen, the woollen industry received little Government support, and in contrast to cotton it was slower and later in becoming a mechanised factory industry. On the whole, the woollen weaver did work for customers in his own locality: he made their own yarn into cloth to clothe their families. The number of weavers was considerable because most male clothing and the shawls worn by women were made of wool. Near bigger centres of population such as Edinburgh, cloth was made for sale and Stirling and Hillfoot villages like Alva were centrally situated to serve wider markets in the Lowlands. The knitting of stockings, especially in Aberdeenshire, and the making of carpets were other branches of the woollen industry.

In spite of being mainly a hand industry serving a local market, some processes in the production of woollen cloth were becoming mechanised with small factories being established in the north-east, the Forth valley and the Borders before 1820:

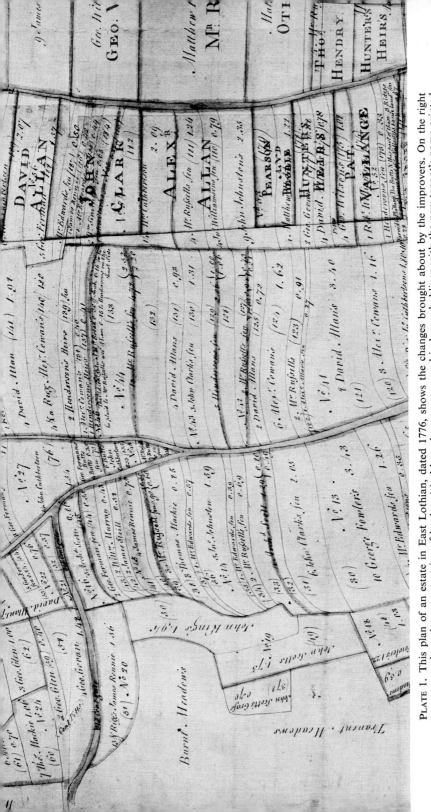

PLATE 1. This plan of an estate in East Lothian, dated 1776, shows the changes brought about by the improvers. On the right you can see how the narrow strips of land or 'rigs' have been re-arranged in larger holdings with the new tenant's name printed in capitals. Find the rigs of one tenant such as David Allan in the centre and left of the plan.

PLATE 2. An early nineteenth-century print of Falkirk with smoke rising from Carron Iron Works in the background. The establishment of the works at Carron was a major milestone in the Scottish Industrial Revolution.

PLATE 3. New Lanark, scene of Dale and Owen's experiments in industrial welfare and co-operation.

PLATE 4. A hewer and women bearers working in a coal seam at Gilmerton Colliery, Midlothian 1786.

PLATE 5. 'Pitlessie Fair' from the painting by Sir David Wilkie.

Customer work

To George Fraiter, weaver in Denholm £ s d
For working 23 yards of coarse flannel 4 2
For working 31 yards of flannel for waistcoats 14 5½

———
18 7½

Border Account Book, 1772

To John Hardie, Stocking-maker in Hawick £ s d
For manufacturing 8 pairs of Stockings 1 1 3
To William Robertson in the Hawick Carpet Factory
For a Small Carpet 5 3

Border Account Book, 1775.

In the 1770's

David Loch's *Essays on the Trade, Commerce, Manufactures and Fisheries of Scotland*, published in 1778, are a valuable source of information on Scottish industry generally. The following extracts have been chosen to show the organisation and some of the processes in the woollen trade:

Stirling has long carried on a very extensive trade in manufacturing shalloons and serges, Highland plaids and carpets. James Young has a neat carpet work. He uses all sorts of wool and gets his yarn spun in the country. Here are about 160 looms, 30 stocking frames, and 17 carpet looms, mostly all in woollen goods.

p. 31.

In Edinburgh, Mr. Archibald M'Dowall employs a great many hands in the woollen branch. His machinery consists of fulling mills, a spinning machine, and such others as are used by those of the same profession in England. He purchases most of his wool at Boswell [St. Boswell's] fair, within four miles of Melrose; and at Edinburgh weigh-house. Mr. Jeeves is among the best blanket-makers in Great Britain. He has often woven thirty yards of cloth a day with the flying shuttle. John Ballantyne, wool merchant, combs weekly twelve Scots stones of wool (at 22 lbs. English per stone). He gives two pence per pound for combing wool and workmen can easily gain one shilling per day if they choose to exert themselves. He dyes every colour to perfection, scarlet excepted.

pp. 2–5.

George Stewart, James Thomson and George Cathie in Musselburgh are good tradesmen and make all kinds of woollen cloths, from two shillings and sixpence to sixteen shillings and sixpence per yard, mostly for the Edinburgh merchants. They all agree that dyeing in the wool is by far the best practice and ought to be encouraged.

pp. 15–16.

The people at Galashiels are all employed in the coarse woollen goods, principally Galashiels' Grey, twenty yards long, value from 1s 6d to 4s per yard. Blankets are likewise made. About 30 looms are employed in this village. The inhabitants spin all their own yarn. There are three waulk-mills that pay six pounds sterling a year to Mr. John Scot of Gala for the water that supplies them.

p. 86.

In Hawick Mr. Robertson and company carry on the carpet manufacture to a large extent, and just now employ 14 looms. Mr. Hardie occupies four frames for stockings and Mr. James Halden two. The number of looms presently employed in linen and woollen is about 65.

pp. 89-90.

Introduced to Hawick by John Hardie in 1771, the stocking industry developed quickly, for by 1816, over five hundred hand-operated frames were in use either in houses or small factory shops.

The Coming of Woollen Mills

The following passages, chosen from the counties of Clackmannan and Moray, show how woollen manufacture was changing:

ALVA : Woollen manufactures have been carried on in the village of Alva for more than a century past. They consist mainly of Scots blankets and serges. The former are made from 9d to 1s the Scots yard, and the latter from 10d to 15d and a few from 16d to 18d per yard. The number of looms employed in the village is 67. The gross produce will amount to from £7,000 to £8,000 annually. The serges are sold not only in Edinburgh but likewise in Stirling, Glasgow, Greenock, Perth and Dundee.

O.S.A., vol. 18, p. 135, Alva, 1796

The making of serges was superseded by the more useful article of plaidings and blanketings, which became the chief commodity after the first woollen factory was built in the year 1798. Since 1826, however, tartan shawls have been introduced and become the most general article manufactured. There are now eight woollen mills.
The number of persons employed is as follows:

in the factories, 149 men   50 women, 81 children
in the village,   89 men 175 women, 21 children

The total of looms is as follows:

looms in the factories   90
looms in the village   80
                        ———

Total   170

N.S.A., vol. 8, pp. 187-8, Alva, 1841

LHANBRYDE: At Newmill, Lhanbryde, near Elgin, the manufacture of woollen cloth has been established in a factory employing fifty people, eight of whom are Yorkshiremen. The whole process of carding and spinning the wool, weaving and dyeing the various colours, dressing and pressing the cloth, is completed in this establishment.

There are also four carding machines chiefly employed in the service of the private families all over the country. The operation of the carding machine is so quick and the wool so much better prepared for being spun, that it is brought in from all the country around, for the distance of nearly twenty miles to be carded by these machines at the rate of 3d per pound.

General View of the Agriculture of Moray and Nairn, p. 401, 1811

1. Name the machines on which (*a*) cloth was woven and (*b*) stockings were knitted.
2. (*a*) James Young of Stirling had his yarn 'spun in the country'. What do you think this means?
   (*b*) Archibald M'Dowall had a spinning machine. Try to find out what spinning machines had been invented by 1778.
   (*c*) Combing was the old hand method of preparing woollen fibres for spinning. How was this done in Lhanbryde in 1811?
   (*d*) Which colour proved difficult to dye?
   (*e*) What is meant by 'dyeing in the wool'? At what other stage in cloth-making might dyeing take place?
   (*f*) What are fulling mills or waulk mills?
3. What changes in the kind of cloth produced in Alva took place (*a*) in the early 1800's and (*b*) after 1826?
4. (*a*) Give the total number of workers in factories in Alva in 1841.
   (*b*) Give the total number of workers in the village in Alva in 1841.
   (*c*) How far had the change-over to factory work gone by that date?
5. On the average, how many workers would a factory in Alva have in 1841? And how many looms?

To guide your writing.

1. How were the lives of (*a*) workers who entered the new factories and (*b*) domestic textile workers changed by the introduction of the factory system? (See also the earlier sections on textiles.)
2. Describe the making of a piece of woollen cloth in the 1770's.
3. Write a survey of the main changes in the textile industries between 1760 and 1820, making reference to the source material in this and the previous two sections.

The Making of Iron

Until the eighteenth century, charcoal was the only fuel commonly used to produce the intense heat which was necessary for smelting iron ore. As supplies of wood for making charcoal became scarce in England, some small ironworks were established in the Highlands of Scotland because of the timber there.

The establishment of the Carron Iron Works near Falkirk in 1759 marked a great advance in the production of ironware in Scotland. From the beginning, it was a large industrial enterprise, and skilled men were brought from England to teach the Scottish workers the processes of producing pig-iron and making articles from iron. Although charcoal was the fuel used for smelting at first, it was soon displaced by coke. A wide variety of articles were manufactured there, including nails, spades, shovels, stoves, grates and cannon.

In spite of the success of Carron, the expansion of the iron industry in Scotland was slow. Several new ironworks were founded, including one at Muirkirk in Ayrshire. It was not until J. B. Neilson invented the hot-blast in 1828 that ironmasters could exploit the blackband ironstone of Monkland parishes, cut fuel costs and produce and sell large quantities of pig-iron at lower prices than their English and Welsh competitors in the 1830's and 40's:

An ironworks using charcoal in the Highlands

The Bonawe furnace on Loch Etive in Argyll stands in a charming situation, embellished around with woods. We learned that it belonged to an English company, who erected works here because of the abundance of wood and water, and its proximity to the sea. The ore used in this foundry was brought in vessels from Cumberland but the woods were beginning to be worked out.

> FAUJAS DE ST. FOND, *Travels in England and Scotland*, vol. 1, p. 148, 1784

The Carron Iron Works

Dr. Roebuck and Mr. Samuel Garbett had established a vitriol works at Prestonpans, which succeeded well and the profits of which encouraged them to undertake the grand ironworks at Carron. Garbett, who was a man of sense and judgement, was much against that great undertaking, as, independent of the profits of the vitriol works, they had not £3,000 stock between them. But the ardent mind of Roebuck carried Garbett away and he yielded. Roebuck, having been bred in the medical school of Edinburgh, had science, and particularly the skill of applying chemistry to the useful arts.

Ironworks were but recent in Scotland, and Roebuck had visited them all, and every station where they could be erected, and had found that Carron was by far the best, which if they did not occupy immediately, some other company would.

DR. ALEXANDER CARLYLE, *Autobiography*, p. 382

The third partner was a Scottish merchant, William Cadell.

The place was covered with cannons, mortars, bombs, balls and those large pieces which they call carronades. Under the sheds where the finished articles are deposited we saw several rows of rampart cannon, battering guns and field pieces destined for Russia and the Emperor. They were longer than usual, of the most perfect workmanship, and covered with a thin varnish of a steel colour to preserve them from rust.

Four furnaces, for melting the ore, devoured both day and night enormous masses of coals and ore. Each disgorges every six hours, streams of liquid iron. Each furnace is supplied by four air pumps, where the air, compressed into iron cylinders, uniting into one pipe, and directed towards the flame, produces a sharp whistling noise and so violent a tremor that one could hardly avoid a feeling of terror.

The coal employed here consists of large lumps. At Carron the operation of converting it into coke takes place in the open air. A quantity of coal is placed on the ground in a round heap, of from 12 to 15 feet in diameter and about two feet in height. As many as possible of the large pieces are set on end, to form passages for the air. As the fire spreads, the mass increases in bulk, swells up, becomes spongy and light, cakes into one body, and at length loses its bitumen, and emits no more smoke. It then acquires a red uniform colour, inclining a little to white, in which state it begins to crack and split open.

At this moment, the heap must be quickly covered with ashes to deprive it of air, similar to the process used in making charcoal.

FAUJAS DE ST. FOND, *Travels*, vol. 1, pp. 177–86, 1784

The poet, Robert Burns, was less impressed, because he failed even to gain entry to the Works but he, it appears, arrived on a Sunday without giving notice to the owners and without revealing who he was. His lines on Carron are well-known:

> We cam na here to view your works
> In hopes to be mair wise
> But only, lest we gang tae hell
> It may be nae surprise.

Carronades

These cannon were effective weapons on both sea and land. Nelson's ships were armed with them and the Duke of Wellington demanded them in the wars against Napoleon:

'My dear Sir,

I have received your letter of the 31st January. I have had enough of sieges with defective artillery and will never undertake another without the best. Therefore in all my letters I have desired to have either 29-pounders, 9 feet long, Carron manufacture or 28-pounders, 8 feet long of the same manufacture, and Carron shot.'

Letter of the DUKE OF WELLINGTON to Admiral Berkeley, 1811

1. (*a*) What attracted English companies to establish ironworks in the Highlands?
   (*b*) What were the disadvantages of producing iron there?
2. What is the meaning of: vitriol; carronades; charcoal; coke; bitumen?
3. Who were the three partners who founded the Carron Iron Works?
4. At Carron where did men make (*a*) coke and (*b*) iron?

Later ironworks

Muirkirk in Ayrshire has been chosen here as an example of an ironworks established later than Carron. Two descriptions are given, one in the 1790's, and the other fifty years later. It should be noted that the amount of coal required here to smelt iron is high, compared with the economies resulting from the use of the hot-blast elsewhere, which produced a ton of pig iron with little over two tons of coal:

The value of property is much increased: a sheep farm, for instance, which a few years ago was bought for £300, within this twelve month gave 1,000 guineas. The rise is not owing to the advanced improvements in agriculture or to any material change of the soil, but the discovery, and expectation of further discovering, of those useful minerals which even the most barren spots cover and contain, and which are so necessary for the manufactures lately established here.

There are two considerable manufactures, iron and coal-tar. The commencement of the former was in the year 1787, and the furnace began to blow in July 1789. There are the most favourable appearances in the necessary articles of coal, ironstone and lime.

O.S.A., vol. 7, pp. 602, 607, Muirkirk

The iron works consists of three large blast furnaces, although two only have been working for a number of years, an extensive forge for making bar-iron, with a foundry and inferior works. These employ about 400 workmen, who work six days in the week and eight hours per day. The materials used in making iron are ironstone, coal and lime, and it takes 2 tons 12 cwt. of ironstone, 8 tons 12 cwt. of coals and 19¾ cwt. of lime to make one ton of pig iron. Founders esteem it soft, easily melted, and of the best quality. The bar-iron is also very superior, being little if at all inferior to the best Swedish iron. This proceeds partly from the coals used in manufacturing it being nearly free of sulphur, and partly from the manner of beating out the bars, instead of drawing them out by rollers as in other iron-works.

N.S.A., vol. 5, p. 155, Muirkirk

1. What effect did the discovery of iron-ore at Muirkirk have on the value of property there?
2. Name the three materials needed for the production of pig iron.
3. What is bar-iron and why was Muirkirk's bar-iron considered to be of good quality?

To guide your writing.
1. Describe the production of iron at Carron and the range of articles manufactured there.
2. (*a*) What advantages did the Carron Iron Works have over the iron establishments in the Highlands?
   (*b*) What effect was the foundation of Carron likely to have on them?
3. What new skills and occupations did the iron industry introduce to Scotland?
4. Using the sources, trace the expansion of the iron industry in Scotland between 1760 and 1830.

The Use of Steam Power

The Steam Engine

Had Watt, at the outset of his career, announced to mankind that he would invent a power which should drain their mines, blow their furnaces, roll and hammer their metals, drive their looms and spindles, print their books, impel ships across the ocean and perform the thousand offices in which steam is now regularly employed, he would have been regarded as an enthusiast, if not as a madman. Yet all this the steam engine has done and is now doing.

SAMUEL SMILES, *Lives of the Engineers*, vol. 4, p. 408

James Watt, a native of Greenock, trained as an instrument maker in Glasgow and London but, not being a burgess, he was not allowed to set up in business in Glasgow. Instead, he became instrument maker to the University. One of the tasks given him there by Professor John Anderson was to examine and put in working order a model of Thomas Newcomen's pumping engine. This was his introduction to the problems of constructing efficient steam engines and adapting them to different uses, which were to occupy his thoughts for most of his working life. The first improvement he made was to use a *separate condenser*:

It was *in the Green of Glasgow*. I had gone to take a walk on a fine Sabbath afternoon. I was thinking upon the engine at the time and had gone as far as the Herd's house when *the idea came into my mind, that as steam was an elastic body it would rush into a vacuum, and if a communication was made between the cylinder and an exhausted vessel, it would rush into it, and might be there condensed without cooling the cylinder. I had not walked further than the Golf-house when the whole thing was arranged in my mind.*

James Watt's account to Robert Hart, in
H. W. DICKINSON, *James Watt*, p. 36, 1936

The prospect of a more economical steam engine won for James Watt the support of Dr. Roebuck, one of the owners of the Carron Iron Company, who financed the construction of an experimental engine at Kinneil Colliery, near Bo'ness. Watt secured a patent for his engine in 1769, and immediately an offer of help came from Matthew Boulton, a shrewd Birmingham businessman, who could see the financial prospects of exploiting Watt's engine:

'I was excited by two motives to offer you my assistance, which were love of you and love of a money-getting ingenious project. I presumed that your engine would require money, very accurate workmanship and extensive correspondence to make it turn out to the best advantage. My idea was to settle a manufactory near to my own by the side of our canal where I would erect all the conveniences necessary for the completion of engines, and from which manufactory we would serve all the world with engines of all sizes. By these means and your assistance we would engage and instruct some excellent workmen (with more excellent tools than would be worth any man's while to procure for a single engine), could execute the invention 20 per cent cheaper than it would be otherwise executed, and with as great a difference of accuracy as there is between the blacksmith and the mathematical instrument maker. It would not be worth my while to make [engines] for three counties only, but I find it very well worth my while to make for all the world.'

Letter of Matthew Boulton to Watt, 1769, quoted by
H. W. DICKINSON, in *James Watt*, p. 52

Watt did not take up Boulton's offer until it became clear to him that Dr. Roebuck lacked the money and Scottish workmen the experience to manufacture his invention. He moved south to join Boulton in Birmingham in 1774. Boulton determined not to sell the engines outright;

instead he charged a royalty for their use, one-third of the value of the fuel saved by using the Boulton and Watt engine compared with the Newcomen engine over a period of twenty-five years. In 1776 the first Boulton and Watt engine was installed in a colliery in Dudley, not far from their Soho Works in Birmingham and Boulton was offering to build steam engines elsewhere, including at the Carron Iron Works. Many were erected to pump water out of coal-mines and another Scot, William Murdock, the pioneer of gas-lighting, assembled several of them in tin-mines in Cornwall. Later, many came into use in Scotland:

On Friday last a Steam Engine constructed by Mr. Watt's new Principles was set to work at Bloomfield Colliery, near Dudley in the Presence of its Proprietors and a Number of Scientific Gentlemen whose Curiosity was excited to see the first Movements of so singular and so powerful a Machine; and whose Expectations were fully gratified by the Excellence of its performance. The Workmanship of the Whole did not pass unnoticed nor unadmired. All the Iron Foundry Parts were executed by Mr. John Wilkinson; the Condenser with the Valves, Pistons and all the small Work at Soho, and the Whole was erected under the Directions of Mr. James Watt.

From the first Movement of its setting to Work, it emptied the Engine Pit (which is about 90 feet deep and stood 57 Feet high in Water) in less than an hour. This Engine is applied to the working of a Pump 14 Inches and a Half Diameter, which it is capable of doing to a depth of 300 Feet, or even 360 if wanted, with one Fourth of the Fuel that a common Engine would require to produce the same Quantity of Power. The liberal Spirit shown by the Proprietors of Broomfield in ordering this, the first large Engine of the Kind that hath ever been made, entitles them to the Thanks of the Public.

Birmingham Gazette, 11th March, 1776

We are desirous to avail ourselves of that Fame which Carron hath so justly acquired by erecting an Engine there.

We are ambitious to convince the proprietors of that manly establishment of the real degree of merit of our Engine as well as of our Dispositions to promote their interest by every means in our power.

Letter of Matthew Boulton, 1776, quoted by
R. H. CAMPBELL, *Carron Company*, p. 44

Watt tackled the problem of converting the backward and forward movement of the piston in the cylinder to rotary motion, which adapted the engine to many new uses in industry, such as driving machinery in textile mills and operating forge hammers. This invention, which many think was really William Murdock's idea, is called *sun and planet*

motion and in the diagram, wheel B represents the planet revolving round
wheel A, the sun, and driving it:

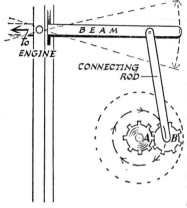

'I have tried a model of one of my old plans of rotative engines revived and executed by W. Murdock. I shall send a drawing and description next post. It has the singular property of going twice round for each stroke of the engine. The wheel *A* is fixed on the end of an axis which carries a fly[wheel]. The wheel *B* is fixed fast to the connecting rod from the working beam and cannot turn on its axis, and is always in contact with wheel *A*. Consequently by the action of the engine it goes round it and causes it to revolve on its axis, and if the wheels are equal in the number of their teeth, *A* will make two revolutions while *B* goes once round it.'

Letter of James Watt to Matthew Boulton, 1782, quoted by
H. W. DICKINSON, *James Watt*, p. 128, 1936

We visited the little garret at Heathfield [Watt's home in England] in which he pursued the investigations of his later years. Everything lay very much as he left it. The piece of iron he was last employed in turning was still in the lathe. The ashes of the last fire were in the grate.

Here are Watt's ladles for melting lead, his foot-rule, his glue-pot, his hammer. There are quadrant glasses, compasses, scales, weights, and boxes of mathematical instruments, once highly prized. In one place is a model of the governor, in another of the parallel motion.

SAMUEL SMILES, *Lives of the Engineers*, vol. 4, pp. 408–9

1. How did Watt's invention of the separate condenser improve the steam engine?
2. What is: a cylinder; a patent; a royalty; rotary motion?
3. (*a*) What were Matthew Boulton's motives for offering help to James Watt?
   (*b*) What advantages was Watt liable to gain by moving south to Birmingham?
4. (*a*) On what financial terms did Boulton and Watt supply steam engines to their customers?
   (*b*) Judging from the amount of fuel mentioned in the account of the Bloomfield Colliery demonstration, would the proprietors expect to save money by installing it?

(c) What task was the engine used for at Bloomfield?

(d) Why was Boulton keen to persuade Carron Company to install one of Watt's engines?

5. Watt was an instrument maker by training but try to suggest a better name for his profession later in his career.

Steamships

Practically all the ships in service until 1820 were sailing ships but inventors were beginning to contemplate the steam-driven ship. Now that the steam engine could produce rotary motion, it could surely be applied to turn paddle-wheels to propel a ship. William Symington was involved in experiments to this end, first along with Patrick Miller on Dalswinton Loch in Dumfries-shire, and later on the Forth and Clyde Canal. As Symington records below, the trial of his ship, the *Charlotte Dundas*, on the Canal in 1802 was successful but the waves it caused made the owners fear for the safety of the banks of the Canal!

Ten years later, Henry Bell's *Comet* made its first voyage on the Clyde, to begin the first regular steamer service in Europe. Soon a new industry was thriving on the banks of the Clyde, the building of ships which were powered by steam. In this way, Clydeside benefited from the improvements first made on the steam engine by a Greenock man, James Watt:

On 14th October, 1788, a boat was put in motion upon Mr. Miller's piece of water at Dalswinton. For some time past his attention had been turned to the use of the steam engine for purposes of navigation. He has now shown to the world the practicability of this by executing it upon a small scale. A vessel of 25 feet long and seven broad was driven with two wheels by a small engine. It answered Mr. Miller's expectations fully and afforded great pleasure to the spectators. The engine used is Mr. Symington's new patent engine.

JAMES TAYLOR, *Dumfries Journal*

I made the *Charlotte Dundas* take in drag two loaded vessels, the *Active* and *Euphemia* of Grangemouth, each vessel upwards of seventy tons burden, and with great ease they were carried, without assistance of any horses, through the summit level of this canal to Port Dundas, a distance of nineteen and a half miles in six hours, although it blew so strong a breeze right ahead that no other vessel in the canal attempted to move to windward. This experiment not only satisfied me but every person who witnessed it of the utility of steam navigation.

William Symington, 1802, quoted by G. PRATT INSH, *Scotland and the Modern World*, pp. 149–51

The Steamboat *Comet*

Between Glasgow, Greenock and Helensburgh

For Passengers Only

The subscriber, having at much expense, fitted up a handsome vessel to ply upon the river Clyde from Glasgow, to sail by the power of air, wind and steam, intends that the vessel shall leave the Broomielaw on Tuesdays, Thursdays, and Saturdays about mid-day, or such an hour thereafter as may suit the state of the tide and to leave Greenock on Mondays, Wednesdays and Fridays in the morning to suit the tide.

The terms are for the present fixed at 4s for the best cabin and 3s for the second.

The subscriber continues his establishment at Helensburgh Baths (Hotel) and a vessel will be in readiness to convey passengers by the *Comet* from Greenock to Helensburgh.

Henry Bell

5th Aug, 1812

Glasgow Chronicle, 12th Aug. 1812

In 1812, our first steamer, the tiny *Comet* with a draught of only four feet, grounded at Renfrew, although Henry Bell was careful to regulate her time of sailing so as to avoid low water. This was told to me by Mrs. Bell who was on board at the time. 'And what was to be done then?', I asked. 'Oh,' was the reply, 'the men just stepped over the side and pushed her across the shoal.'

ANDREW MACGEORGE, *Old Glasgow*, p. 245, 1880

1. Name the two men responsible for the first steam-powered ship.
2. What did the experiment on the Forth and Clyde Canal require the *Charlotte Dundas* to do and how successful was it?
3. Besides his own interest in steam-navigation, what reason did Henry Bell have for starting a steamer service on the Clyde?

To guide your writing.

1. (*a*) Which industries benefited from the improved steam engine?
   (*b*) How did it affect men's working lives?
2. The separate condenser, sun and planet motion, parallel motion and the governor are four main inventions associated with the name of James Watt. Try to find out more about the last two, and then write an account of his contribution to the development of steam power.
3. Write an account of the part played by Scots in promoting steamships before 1820.

4·STANDARDS OF LIVING

Workers in the Country

To tell whether a man is poor or well-off, his income must be considered in relation to his necessary expenditure, which depends partly on the size of his family and partly on the level of prices at the time. People are inclined to make other comparisons, with other people's incomes, for example, or with their own incomes at an earlier time and many yearn for the lower prices they remember in their younger days.

Ideally it would be useful to study the wages of as many occupations as possible, and the prices of as many common articles as possible, for every ten, or even twenty, years between 1760 and 1820 (but even these would not take account of exceptional years in between, e.g. years of famine and very high prices). Such ideal figures are not available to us but much interesting information can be culled from the volumes of the *Old* and *New Statistical Accounts* to help us to construct a picture of the standard of living of people at this time:

Wages, rents and prices in Perthshire

	Wages 1772	1792	1837
Man-servant's average yearly wages, excluding food	£3 6s 8d	£10 10s 0d	£12 12s 0d
Maid-servant's average yearly wages, excluding food	£2 2s 0d	£3 3s 0d	£6 0s 0d
Best labourer's hire per day	9d	1s 0d	1s 10d
Mason's hire per day	1s 2d	1s 8d	2s 6d
House carpenter's hire per day	1s 1d	1s 6d	2s 2d
Rents			
Highest rent of land, near the town, per acre	10s 0d	£2 17s 0d	£6 0s 0d
Lowest rent of land, near the town, per acre	—	—	£2 2s 0d
Average rent of land, in the country, per acre	5s 0d	12s 0d	£1 10s 0d
Prices			
Average price of cheese per stone in summer	3s 0d	3s 6d	3s 6d

	1772	1792	1837
Average price of cheese per stone in winter	4s 8d	5s 4d	4s 0d
Average price of butter per lb.	6d	8d	10d
Average price of best beef and veal per lb.	3d	4d	5d
Average price of best mutton per lb.	2d	3d	5d
Average price of fowls a piece	6d	9d	1s 3d
Average price of dozen of eggs	2d	3d	7d
Average price of coals per stone	2d	3d	2½d

N.S.A., vol. 10, pp. 512–13, Crieff, Perthshire

1. (a) What general change took place in (i) wages (ii) rents and (iii) prices, between the dates given?
   (b) What exceptions to the general trend can you find?
   (c) Which of the workers has had his or her wages increased most (i) between 1772 and 1792 and (ii) between 1792 and 1837?
2. Taking into account changes in both wages and prices, do you think people were better off (a) in 1792 compared with 1772 and (b) in 1837 compared with 1792?

Allowances of ploughmen

The manservant, probably a ploughman, was not paid in money only, but had other allowances of food, footwear and clothing as the report on Alloa in O.S.A., vol. 8, p. 626 shows:

Perquisites of ploughmen.	
4 ells of grey cloth at 1s per ell	4s 0d
6 ells of coarse linen for shirts at 6d per ell	3s 0d
2 ells of plaiding, or coarse flannel at 10d per ell	1s 8d
2 pairs of shoes	5s 0d
	13s 8d = value in 1760

A 'household ploughman' also had his food provided in the farmer's house, while an 'outdoor ploughman' who did not 'live in' was given 6½ bolls of meal a year and had the right to grow 2–3 pecks of potatoes.

1. Try to find out the meaning of: perquisite; ell; 'live in'; boll; peck.

Income and expenditure of a day labourer

The minister of Caputh in Perthshire in 1793 supplied this detailed account of the income and expenditure of a poor family in his parish. The husband, a day labourer, and his wife had four children, all under seven years of age:

Earnings a week:

The man earns, at a medium	5s	9d
The woman earns by spinning	2s	0d
Total	7s	9d
Amount in the year £20	3s	0d

Expenses a week

Four pecks of oatmeal and two of barley-meal	4s	6d
Milk, fat, onions and potatoes	1s	1d
Soap, starch, blue and oil		3d
Butter, cheese, bacon or other meat		6d
Thread and worsted		1d
Total	6s	5d
Amount in the year £16	13s	8d
Excess of earnings £3	9s	4d

Annual Expenses

The man's wear of a suit 4s; of a working jacket and breeches 4s; of a bonnet and handkerchief 1s 1d	9s	1d
Of two shirts 8s; of a pair of shoes and two pairs of stockings 9s	17s	0d
The woman's wear of gown and petticoats 4s; of a shift 3s 3d	7s	3d
Of a pair of shoes 4s; and a pair of stockings 1s 6d	5s	6d
Of an apron 1s 6d; of handkerchiefs, caps, etc. 3s	4s	6d
The children's wear	15s	0d
Lying in, loss of time by sickness and bad weather, and burials, one year with another	11s	0d
	£3 9s	4d

Rent of house and garden £1. The garden which the man dresses in the mornings and evenings affords the family cabbages, greens and potatoes, to the amount of the rent. Fuel costs 10s; but after dunging the garden, there is a remainder of ashes, which dungs as much ground (given by the farmer) as produces potatoes worth 10s.

O.S.A., vol. 9, p. 500, Caputh 1793

There is an example also of a weaver's family who are better off and end an average year with a surplus of £2 6s 10d.

Note that, after paying his weekly expenses and annual expenses, the day labourer has not a penny left. His rent is £1 extra but the potatoes, etc. which he grows in his garden are worth that amount and are included in 'expenses a week' under the item, 'milk, fat, onions, potatoes'. To pay for fuel he probably sold some potatoes.

1. Are the day labourer's wages similar to those in Crieff parish in the 1790's?
2. What were the main items of food for this labourer's family and what foods could they afford to spend only a little money on?

The Rise in the Standard of Living

One person who had no doubt that the standard of living of country folk had risen a great deal between 1760 and 1790 was the minister of Mains of Fintry in Angus who commented in 1793, 'the inhabitants enjoy the comforts of life to a considerable degree'. He provided the following evidence, based on careful observation, to show how their wealth had increased in terms of food, dress and material goods:

1760	1790
The wages of men servants, that followed the plough were £3 a year; of maid servants £1 10s 0d.	Men servants' wages are £8, some £10; maid servants £4.
No English cloth was worn except by the minister and a Quaker.	There are few who do not wear English cloth: several the best superfine; cotton vests are common.
There were only two hats in the parish; the men wore cloth bonnets.	Few bonnets are worn; the bonnet-maker trade in the next parish is given up.
The women wore coarse plaids: not a cloak, nor bonnet was worn by any woman in the whole parish.	Cotton stockings are worn by both sexes both masters and servants; some have silk ones; the women who wear plaids have them fine and faced with silk; silk plaids, cloaks and bonnets are very numerous.
There was only one eight-day clock in the parish, six watches and one tea-kettle.	There are 30 clocks, above 100 watches, and at least 160 tea-kettles, there being scarce a family but hath one and many that have two.

PLATE 6. The younger members of a Highland village find relaxation in dancing. Providing the music in this painting by David Allan are Neil Gow and his brother, Donald.

PLATE 7. Some idea of the formal attire worn by a landed family of the period can be gauged from this painting of Sir John Halkett of Pitfarrons, Bt., his Wife and Family by David Allan.

The people never visited each other but at Xmas. The entertainment was broth and beef; the visitors sent to an alehouse for five or six pints of ale, and were merry over it without any ceremony.

People visit each other often; a few neighbours are invited to one house to dinner, six or seven dishes are set on the table, elegantly dressed; after dinner a large bowl of rum punch is drunk; then tea, again another bowl; after that supper, and what they call the grace drink.

Children at school had a piece of pease bread in their pockets for dinner.

Children at school have wheaten bread, sweet milk, butter, cheese, eggs and sometimes roast meat.

O.S.A., vol. 5, pp. 226–8, Mains of Fintry

To guide your writing.
1. (*a*) Write an account of the changes in the standard of living of people living in the country between 1760 and 1837, paying attention to people's occupations and wages, prices and what people spent money on.
   (*b*) Try to explain why these changes took place.
   (*c*) Compare the income of the Caputh labourer with the allowances for the unemployed poor in The Church's Responsibility for the Poor on page 96.
2. Write a paragraph to prove that people in Mains of Fintry were better off in 1790.
3. Study the reports on your own parish in the *Old* and *New Statistical Accounts* and see what you can find out about the people's standard of living.

Workers in Industry

Wages

When industries began, they had to compete for workers against traditional occupations like farm-work. Small farmers, displaced by improving landlords, and Highlanders from over-populated areas might be attracted by the prospect of any job but whether a ploughman or an outdoor tradesman would change over to factory work would depend on the conditions and wages offered. Here are some examples of wages paid to industrial workers:

AT CRAMOND IRON WORKS: Here, above thirty men and boys are

c

employed, some of whom earn 26s per week, and none make less than 4s. There are also here spade, nail and file manufacturers. These three branches employ about fifty men and boys, who make from 3s to 20s per week.

O.S.A., vol. 1, p. 213, Cramond

AT ADELPHI COTTON MILL near Doune, where 700 people were employed in the 1790's:

The workmen are paid by the quantity and quality of their work, and hence they have become extremely dexterous and some hands will make about two guineas a week.

At the same time, tradesmen in the parish were earning less:

Mason's Work:

Master per week	15s 0d
Journeyman per week	12s 0d
Labourer per week	7s 6d

Slater's work:

Master per week	15s 0d
Journeyman per week	14s 0d

O.S.A., vol. 20, pp. 87, 96, Doune

IN COAL-MINES: A collier, with his wife and daughter, earns 12s in five days, which is all the time he works in the week. Besides this he has his meal from the proprietor at 8½d per peck; a free house and yard and other bounties to the amount of 30s yearly.

O.S.A., vol. 14, p. 622, Clackmannan

The colliers could not leave their work, but an old collier who was past labour, was allowed two pecks of meal per week, and he had his free house and garden, and likewise his firing, continued to him, the same as when working. Each collier has a free house and garden, a quantity of meal, proportioned to the number of the family at the rate of 10½d per peck, and their firing. Each family, upon an average, consumes rather more than 7 cwt. of coal a week. The colliers are paid by the piece: a good collier can clear from £25 to £35 per annum. To the women and children who carry up the coals on their backs, the colliers pay 4d for carrying 30 cwt.

O.S.A., vol. 8, p. 615, Alloa

From the passing of this Act, all the Colliers in that Part of Great Britain called Scotland, who are bound Colliers, shall be and they are hereby declared to be free from their servitude.

Act of Parliament, 1799

Generally, how do wages of industrial workers compare with those of:

(a) ploughmen (see previous section) and (b) tradesmen?

2. (a) What additional benefits did a collier have besides wages?

(b) When did colliers gain their freedom?

Child Labour

IN MINES: Ann Waugh, aged sixteen, a putter, had worked in the pit for eight years:

I work on the long days, fifteen and sixteen hours; two in the morning till five and six at night. On the short days only eight hours as the engine only works three days a week. I draw in harness and sister hangs on and pushes behind. The work is gai sair and we often get knocked down as the cart descends the brae. The cart holds 5 cwt. of coal.

Evidence to the Children's Employment Commission, 1842, quoted by R. H. CAMPBELL in *Carron Company*, p. 229

AT HAND-WEAVING: Is it the general practice in Scotland to put children under ten years of age to hand-weaving? – It is universally the practice.

And to bind them apprentices? – Yes.

For how long? – Various periods, three, four and five years, according to the age and circumstances of the parties.

Is that work hard labour? – For children of that age it is much harder labour than any employment that children under fourteen can have in cotton factories.

ADAM BOGLE, manager of Blantyre cotton mill to the *Committee on the State of Children Employed in Manufactories*, 1816, p. 169

IN COTTON MILLS: David Dale's spinning mills at New Lanark were the biggest in Scotland and many children were employed there. As will be seen from his answers, his care for the health and education of the children who worked for him was exceptional and conditions there should not be regarded as typical of factories at that time:

Queries submitted to Mr. Dale of Glasgow by Mr. Bayley of Manchester, in connection with Working Conditions in the Mills at New Lanark (1796).

Hours of labour, of rest and for meals?

The hours of labour are eleven and a half each day, from six o'clock in the morning till seven o'clock at night, with half an hour at nine o'clock for breakfast and a whole hour at two for dinner.

Time and manner of teaching the children to read, and of religious instruction?

The teaching commences at 7.30 and continues till nine o'clock. The schools at present are attended by five hundred and seven scholars, in instructing whom sixteen teachers are employed. On Sundays that part of the children who cannot go to church for want of accommodation are kept busy at school; and in the evenings after public worship, the usual teachers spend regularly three hours in giving religious instruction.

Besides the night schools there are two day schools for children too young to work, which, as well as the night one (except for providing their own books) are entirely free of expense to the scholars.

Mode and time of hiring?

Those who agree for a stipulated weekly wage, and who are generally such as live with their parents, are commonly engaged for four years; while such as are received from the workhouse in Edinburgh or who are otherwise without friends to take charge of them, and who, instead of wages, are maintained and educated, are bound four, five, six or seven years, according to their age, or generally till they have completed their fifteenth year. The mode of hiring is generally by contract of the parents or curators of the children in their behalf.

Where do the workers come from?

They come either from the native inhabitants of the place; from families who have been collected about the works from the neighbouring parishes, and more distant parts of the country; or lastly from Edinburgh or Glasgow, by the number of destitute children these places constantly afford.

Mode of lodging and feeding the children?

Those who get their maintenance instead of wages, are lodged all together in one house. They consist at present of 396 boys and girls. There are six sleeping apartments for them, and three children are allowed to each bed.

The upper body clothing in use in summer, both for boys and girls, is entirely of cotton; in winter the boys are dressed in woollen cloth, and they, as well as the girls have complete dress suits for Sundays. For a few months in summer both boys and girls go without shoes or stockings.

They have oatmeal porridge for breakfast and supper, and milk with it in its season. For dinner every day they have barley broth made from fresh beef. The beef itself is divided among one half of the children, in quantities of about seven ounces English to each; the other half is served with cheese, in quantities of about five ounces English each; so that they have alternately beef and cheese for dinner, excepting now and then a dinner of herrings in winter and fresh butter in summer. They also have a plentiful allowance of potatoes or barley bread, and more every morning before going to work.

Are they commonly strong for labour?

The workers are as strong and robust as others. The male part of them are fit for any trade. A great many, since the commencement of the war, have gone into the army and navy, and others [become] apprentices to smiths and joiners, etc., but especially to weavers. The females generally leave the mills and go to private family service when about sixteen years of age.

> Quoted by T. FERGUSON, *The Dawn of Scottish Social Welfare*, pp. 93–6

When Robert Owen, David Dale's son-in-law, gained control of New Lanark, he made further improvements. Young children were not allowed to work in the mills but went to school until they were ten years old. For children at work, hours were reduced to ten and three-quarters per day and they attended school in the evening. Besides the teaching of reading, writing and arithmetic, Owen was keen on giving the children plenty of exercise but not everyone shared his enthusiasm for it, as the following extract shows:

I asked her what made her leave [New] Lanark. She said it was with a view of bettering her situation; she had been better before, and she thought she might be better still; that there had been a number of new regulations introduced. That they had got a number of dancing-masters, a fiddler, a band of music, that there were drills and exercises, and that they were dancing together till they were more fatigued than if they were working.
Did the woman complain that she got no wages for the dancing?
No.

> ADAM BOGLE, manager of Blantyre cotton mill, to the *Committee on the State of Children Employed in Manufactories*, 1816, p. 167

1. How long did children work per day and how long did they spend in school in New Lanark in David Dale's time?
2. What happened about children who were too young for work?
3. (*a*) How many workhouse or destitute children were employed by David Dale?
   (*b*) How well were they provided for?
4. Why did the woman who left New Lanark complain?

To guide your writing.
1. Write a conversation between a mason's labourer and a cotton worker at Adelphi mill on the subject of the wages they earn.
2. Explain why a farm worker, a labourer, or even an outdoor tradesman might (*a*) prefer to work in a factory but (*b*) be less willing to become a miner in the late eighteenth century.
3. If you were a reformer at that time what would you want to do

(*a*) about Ann Waugh's work in the mine (*b*) child weavers and (*c*) what changes by Robert Owen would you praise and what others would you wish to make at New Lanark?

4. Do you think that other employers would be keen to follow David Dale's and Robert Owen's examples in educating child workers?

Other Men's Spending

For comparison with the standard of living of workers on the land and in industry, details of some expenses of other members of society are given below:

The Lawyer's Hair-dressing Bill

Munro Ross, Esq., Advocate   To Henry Murray,
Hairdresser.

To dressing your hair from Dec. 1776–Dec. '77	£4 4s 0d
To 12 lbs. powder at 1s per lb.	12s 0d
To 2 tortoise shell combs	4s 0d
To 2 teeth brushes	1s 2d
To 8 pair of rollers	2s 0d
To a bag-wig	17s 0d
To instructing your son to dress	£1 1s 0d
	£7 1s 2d

Pitcalnie Papers

The Laird's Funeral

When the great man died, his relatives and servants went into mourning; his tenants and friends who attended his funeral had to be catered for at the funeral dinner. The total cost, not counting food from the house, totalled £140 17s 7½d. Here are some of the more interesting items in the account, dated 1774:

For making tables and seats for the funeral dinner	£1 16s 0d
For bread to the funeral	£6 2s 6d
For digging the grave	10s 6d
For black cloth and mounting for the mourning for men-servants and two women-servants and for black cloth to his seat in the Kirk, pulpit, etc.	£41 4s 11d
For making mournings for Miss ——	15s 10d
For making mournings for the men-servants	£2 16s 7d

Border Account Book, 1774

The Cost of being a Student

Pryse Lockhart Gordon was a student at University in Aberdeen in 1776. Aberdeen had two colleges at this time, King's and Marischal, which were independent of each other and claimed to be separate universities. Scottish universities were much smaller then and their students younger:

Expenses of a journey on foot from Deskford in Banffshire to Aberdeen (fifty miles), performed in two days, with my companion, James Gray	2s 4d
College fees to the bell-ringer and sacrist	5s 0d
My share of coals and candles for the winter	17s 6d
Pens, ink and paper	6s 6d
Breakfast of bread and milk, at the rate of 9d per week (26 weeks)	19s 6d
Board (dinner) at college table, at 14s per month	£4 4s 0d
Bread, cheese, butter, smoked haddocks, small beer and other *luxuries*, for supper	£1 4s 0d
Tea and sugar, once or twice a week	12s 0d
Expenses at taverns and dancing balls	18s 0d
To Sweety Nell, an old woman who sold lollypops	13s 0d
Washing	£1 4s 0d
Expenses at college balls	8s 0d
To the bed-maker	12s 0d
To Squinting Sandy, for cleaning shoes	6s 0d
A pair of gloves at the graduation ball	1s 6d
Sweeties at various times	6s 0d
Three pen-knives (always losing them)	3s 0d
Shuttlecocks	1s 4d
Fine for being late at roll-call	3s 6d
Fine for throwing snowball at the sacrist	6d
Fee to the Greek Professor	£1 11s 6d
Fee to the Professor of Humanity (Latin)	15s 0d
Charity in Church	1s 1d
Charity to beggars	1s 6d
Paid for lessons in drawing	12s 0d
To a Highland sergeant for lessons in the broadsword	6s 0d
Skates and Cudgels	4s 6d
Expenses of returning home (partly by coach)	5s 0d
	£17 4s 3d

My grandfather thought me very extravagant, observing that his expenses never exceeded twelve pounds per session: but that was *sixty years* before.

Pryse Lockhart Gordon, Personal Memoirs, quoted in J. G. FYFE'S *Scottish Diaries and Memoirs*, 1746–1843

To guide your writing.

1. Notice the difference between the cost of cloth for mournings at the laird's funeral and the tailor's bill for making them up. What changes have since taken place in the cost of labour compared with material, and why?
2. If this student's grandfather thought he was extravagant, which items of expenditure do you think he would criticise?
3. Using the student's expenses as evidence, give an account of his life at university, mentioning (*a*) the college classes he attended (*b*) other lessons he took and (*c*) his pleasures and recreations.
4. Another detailed account of a student's expenses by Duncan Dewar, a Perthshire student of St. Andrews, between 1819 and 1827, has been edited by P. Scott Lang. If you can find a copy you should be able to make an interesting comparison of the lives of two students attending different universities at different times.
5. Do you think it is possible to draw any conclusions about rich and poor in the late eighteenth century compared with the present day, and if so, what are your conclusions?

5·IMPROVED COMMUNICATIONS IN THE LOWLANDS

Roads

Until the middle of the eighteenth century roads worthy of the name hardly existed in Scotland, except for the military roads constructed in the Highlands by General Wade and his successors, and even these soon fell into disrepair. Road maintenance was done by farm tenants who were forced to work on them for up to six days a year (see the Aberdeen-shire tenant's letter on page 8). This was called statute labour because it was imposed by statute or Act of Parliament in 1669.

That this method did not provide good roads is clear from many accounts of the difficulties of inland travel and transport at the time. Few people travelled very far: a poor man would walk, while a rich man would ride on horseback but coaches could seldom be used. Goods were usually carried on pack-horses. Rivers were the greatest barriers to communication between one place and another. In towns which had grown up at suitable crossing-points there were bridges, but these were often quite narrow and a traveller might have to travel miles along a river before he came to a bridge. Often people had to rely on fords or ferries, and in one unusual case, on a man with a pair of stilts:

Difficulties in Crossing Rivers

New Brig (completed in 1788) to the Auld Brig:

Will your poor, narrow foot-path of a street
Where twa wheel-barrows tremble where they meet
Your ruined formless bulk o' stane and lime
Compare wi' bonnie Brigs o' modern time?

ROBERT BURNS, *The Brigs o' Ayr*

No bridge over the Tay at Dunkeld or over the Spey at Fochabers or over the Findhorn at Forres. Nothing but wretched ferries, pierless, let to poor cottars, who rowed or pushed or hawled a crazy boat across, or more commonly got their wives to do it.

LORD COCKBURN, *Memorials of His Time*, p. 197, 1807

'Ye'll no can wade Yarrow, but Wattie Laidlaw can stilt it when it's gey big and he'll cairry ye ower on his back.' Wattie Laidlaw was at

49

the waterside according to appointment. He gets Janet on his back and her bundle between his teeth and stilts the Yarrow. They landed safely on the other side.

Aunt Janet's Legacy, pp. 55, 62, 1813

This is how a little girl in Selkirkshire went off to her first employment, at an unusually early age for she was not yet eight years old. She was to be cut off from home for eight months by a river she could not cross by herself.

1. According to the New Brig, what was wrong with the Auld Brig in Ayr?
2. Why were ferries poor substitutes for bridges?

The State of the Roads

Nothing was put upon a cart, that could be carried on a horse. Corn and meal, of all kinds, were generally conveyed on horseback, in sacks. Coals were also conveyed on horseback, in a bag containing three hundredweights. Peats, too, were carried on horseback, universally in the vicinity of Edinburgh, even in my own time; so also were straw and hay. There was then a set of single-horse traffickers, under the name of cadgers, that regularly plied on all roads, disposing of many kinds of commodities that were then in demand: as fish, salt, eggs, poultry, and crockery-ware.

In carrying goods from distant towns it was necessary, however, to have a cart, as all that a horse could carry on its back, in a sack or in creels, could not remunerate for the expense of a long journey. The town-carrier had a horse in awkward enough harness, dragging a rudely formed cart through dub and through mire, from one town to another. The time required was longer, but was unavoidable. It is said, and I can well believe it, that the common carrier from Selkirk to Edinburgh, thirty-eight miles distant, required two weeks to make out his journey betwixt the two towns, going and returning, with a suitable resting time at each, to his poor, fatigued horse. The channel of Gala Water itself, when not flooded, was the track chosen, as being the most level, and easiest to be travelled on. The rest of the way, very much up-and-down-hill, was far worse.

GEORGE ROBERTSON, *Rural Recollections*, pp. 39-41, 1829

Whereas the aforesaid roads [between Edinburgh and Glasgow], by the deepness of the soil in some places, and their narrowness and ruggedness in others, are in many parts become impassable in winter for wheel carriages and horses, and very dangerous to travellers, and several bridges upon the said roads are in a ruinous condition, a body of trustees, consisting chiefly of landed proprietors, and including the provost, bailies, etc. of the city of Glasgow was appointed for keeping the roads in proper order with power to erect turnpikes and levy tolls and duties to meet the expenditure.

Act of Parliament, 1753. *Records of Glasgow*, vol. 6, pp. 591–2

1. How were goods transported (*a*) a short distance and (*b*) a long distance?
2. What is the difference between a cadger and a carrier?
3. Why did the Selkirk carrier drive along the channel of Gala Water?
4. What was wrong with the road between Glasgow and Edinburgh and how did Glasgow propose to deal with it?

Turnpike Trusts

Turnpike Trusts, like the one above for Glasgow and district were created by Acts of Parliament, normally making a county the area of administration. Glasgow had one of the earliest Turnpike Trusts and in the next fifty years county after county used this method of providing better roads, although Banffshire did not turn to this system until 1804. The principle adopted was that those who used each stretch of road were to pay for its upkeep, making payment to the toll-keeper who then opened the gate or turnpike to give them access to it. Naturally, travellers were unwilling to pay and complained of the number of toll-houses where payment had to be made. An examination of maps of the period, however, shows that toll-houses were erected on roads leading out of towns and again inside county boundaries. Cases of toll-houses being near one another arose at road junctions or when a traveller was passing from the jurisdiction of one Turnpike Trust to another. The following extracts, although relating to the County of Edinburgh, now Midlothian, are typical of the regulations and charges made elsewhere in Scotland:

The produce of the tolls or duties raised on each road shall be applied towards upholding and repairing that road or building new bridges thereon, where necessary, so as each particular road may have its own produce.

Turnpike Act for the County of Edinburgh, 1751

REGULATIONS

1. Every toll-gatherer shall place on the front of his toll-house his Christian name and surname, painted in black on a board with a white ground, each of the letters of such name to be at least two inches in length.

2. Every toll-gatherer shall place on the front of the toll-house the printed table, containing the name of the toll-bar, with a list of the tolls payable.

3. No toll shall be demanded from any horses or carriages, attending his Majesty or any of the Royal Family, or for any waggon or cart, conveying materials for making or repairing any turnpike roadway, or for any horses or other beasts going to plough, or harrow or to pasture, or from any person going to or returning from their usual place of public worship on Sundays, or from clergymen on parochial duty; or for any beast or carriage employed in conveying the mails of letters under the authority of his Majesty's Post-master General, or for the horse of any officers or soldiers on their march or on duty.

4. Trustees shall have power to widen roads to twenty feet, twenty feet being hereby declared to be the least legal breadth of a turnpike road, and they may widen to a width of forty feet.

5. The Trustees shall cause stones or posts to be set up, on or near the sides of every turnpike road, at a distance of one mile from one another, denoting the distance from some town or place, to or from, which such road shall lead.

6. The owner of every waggon or cart, and of every coach, post-chaise or other carriage let to hire shall paint on its side the Christian name and surname and place of abode of the owner, not less than one inch in height, with numbers, where more than one (carriage) shall belong to the same owner.

General Turnpike Act for Scotland, 1824

COUNTY OF EDINBURGH
TABLE OF TOLLS
1809

1. Stage-coach, drawn by two horses, carrying passengers for hire:

Six inside or under	{ without outside passengers	1s 0d
	{ with outside passengers	1s 8d
Each additional inside passenger		2d

2. Stage-coach drawn by three or more horses, carrying passengers for hire:

	⎰ and not more than two outside passengers	2s 0d
Four inside	⎨ and not more than five outside passengers	3s 0d
	⎱ and above five outside	5s 0d

rising to:

Above ten	⎰ and not more than two outside passengers	4s 8d
inside	⎨ and not more than five outside passengers	5s 4d
	⎱ and above five outside	9s 0d

3. Every other coach, chaise, etc.

Drawn by 1 horse	6d	Drawn by 4 or 5 horses	2s 0d
Drawn by 2 horses	1s 0d	Drawn by 6 horses	3s 0d
Drawn by 3 horses	1s 8d		

4. Waggon, etc. with more than two wheels:

Drawn by 1 horse	6d	Drawn by 4 horses	4s 0d
Drawn by 2 horses	8d	Drawn by 5 horses	6s 0d
Drawn by 3 horses	3s 0d	Drawn by 6 horses	8s 0d

5. Loaded carts with two wheels:

1st For 25 cwt. or under

Drawn by 1 horse	6d
Drawn by 2 or more horses	8d
2nd Above 25 and under 33 cwt.	1s 0d
3rd 33 cwt. and upwards	1s 4d

6. Saddled horse, with or without rider   2d
7. Every other horse laden or unladen   1½d
8. Ass, loaded or not loaded   1d
9. Oxen or cattle per score, and so proportionately:

1st Feb. to 1st Oct.	1s 3d
1st Oct. to 1st Feb.	1s 8d

10. Calves, Hogs, Sheep, Lambs, Goats per score   6d

Varied Rates:

11. Flour from Water of Leith Mills – Half of full rates
12. Every carriage or cart on which the owner's name
ought to be painted but is not – Double toll

General Turnpike Act, Edinburgh, 1824

1. Explain the meaning of: Turnpike Trust; turnpike; toll; stage-coach; per score.
2. Who and what were excused from paying toll?
3. What was the minimum legal breadth of a turnpike road?
4. (*a*) Why do you think owners' names were required on carts and coaches?
   (*b*) Are they still required on commercial vehicles today?
5. (*a*) Study Nos. 1 and 2 in the Table of Tolls and explain the reasons for the different rates charged.
   (*b*) Which vehicles were normally charged the heaviest tolls and why do you think this was?
   (*c*) Which vehicles might be required to pay double toll?
   (*d*) Who paid only half rates?

Improving the Roads

Tolls provided the Turnpike Trusts with an income from which to finance the improvement of the roads under their control. Needless to

say, they wanted this done as cheaply as possible and the methods of
John Loudon Macadam appealed to them in Scotland as well as in
England. Joseph Mitchell, one of Thomas Telford's lieutenants in the
Highlands, probably betrays some professional jealousy when he
criticises Macadam's methods:

It does not matter if the soil be clay, sand, morass or bog; I should
not care whether the substratum was soft or hard; I should prefer a soft
one to a hard one. I never put large stones on the bottom of a road; I
would not put a large stone in any part of it.

> J. L. MACADAM, *Evidence on Highways of the Kingdom*, 1819

The size of stone used on a road must be in due proportion to the space
occupied by a wheel of ordinary dimensions on a smooth level surface.
The point of contact will be found to be, longitudinally, about an inch,
and every piece of stone put into a road, which exceeds an inch in any of
its dimensions, is mischievous.

> J. L. MACADAM, *Remarks on the Present System
> of Roadmaking*, p. 35

Mr. Macadam is aware that in ordinary circumstances, 8 to 10 inches
of well-broken road metal will last from six to ten years in proportion
to the traffic. On acquiring charge of a Turnpike Road therefore, he
saves the expense of quarrying and carting new materials by breaking
up the surface of the road and relaying it in a regular and uniform shape.
In this manner he makes a better road and creates a striking saving of
expense. This continues until the whole stock of materials is exhausted.

> JOSEPH MITCHELL, *Letter to James Hope*, 1833

1. Why did Macadam's roads have a smooth surface?
2. Why were they fairly inexpensive?
3. Why, according to Mitchell, did they not last long?

Travel

Roads improved by the Turnpike Trusts facilitated the transport of
goods by allowing carts and waggons to be used, as the List of Tolls for
the County of Edinburgh shows. They also encouraged people to travel
either in stage-coaches for which they paid a fare like passengers in a bus,
or by hiring a post-chaise for their own use. As travel became faster,
more changes of horses were needed and coaching inns with stables
attached were built on main roads, where horses could be rested and
passengers stay the night:

EDINBURGH TO GLASGOW IN A DAY: The good roads lately made

in many places in Scotland have meant that stage coaches and other carriages are established between Edinburgh and several other towns. A coach sets out every day, Sundays excepted, at eight in the morning from Glasgow and from Edinburgh, and makes the journey from one city to the other in a day; the passengers pay twelve shillings each.

> Scots Magazine, 1756, quoted by L. GARDINER,
> Stage Coach to John o' Groats, p. 29

THE GREAT NORTH ROAD: EDINBURGH FLY (one Day Summer, one and half Winter) from the Black Bull, Newcastle, 5 o'clock morning: Tuesday, Thursday, Saturday to the Black Bull, Edinburgh; 105 miles, £1 11s 6d.

Post Stages with the Distance, Horse and Chaise Hire of each,
as charged on the Road:

Post Stages	Distance	Post-horse	Post-chaise	Post-chaise and 4 horses
		s d	s d	£ s d
Edinburgh to Haddington	16 ml.	4 0	12 0	1 0 0
Haddington to Dunbar	11 ml.	2 9	8 3	13 9
Dunbar to Press Inn	14 ml. 3 fur.	3 6	10 6	17 6
Press Inn to Berwick	11 ml. 3 fur.	3 0	9 0	15 0

> ARMSTRONG, Survey of the Great Post Roads between
> London and Edinburgh, pp. 5, 3, 1776

ROYAL MAIL: In place of on horseback, the mail is conveyed in a carriage with lamps on the back of which is printed EDINBURGH AND GLASGOW ROYAL MAIL. The driver is dressed in a blue coat with a red neck and a helmet. He has a cutlass hung on one side, and a small bugle horn. In front of his seat are two pistols. The mail is put in a box below the seat.

> Edinburgh Advertiser, 1803, quoted by L. GARDINER,
> Stage Coach to John o' Groats, p. 166

1. Which was the cheaper way to travel, by the Edinburgh Fly or by post-chaise?
2. According to Armstrong's Survey how much did it cost per mile to travel from Edinburgh to Haddington (a) by horse (b) by post-chaise and (c) by post-chaise and four horses?
3. Why do you think the driver of the Edinburgh-Glasgow Mail Coach was armed?

To guide your writing.
1. What were the obstacles which made travel and the transport of goods difficult before the formation of Turnpike Trusts?

2. A young coachman is complaining about the high rates of toll to an old carrier in the stable yard of an inn. The carrier points out the advantages of the new roads. Write an account of their conversation.
3. Examine the case for and against Macadam's method of road-making.
4. Study the map of Ayrshire (Fig. 1) and see (a) how many toll houses you can find and (b) if you can find a route from Ayr to Newburn in the north without paying toll.
5. In your own area, look for toll houses or place names which indicate that there used to be toll houses there. Look also for old-established hotels which used to be coaching inns: there is sometimes a garage today where the stables used to be. See if you can reconstruct the local scene by map, drawing or description of the days of Turnpike Trusts.
6. Using the sources here, write an account of the improvement of roads and road transport in the period from 1760 to 1820.

Canals

The ease with which heavy loads could be transported on water compared with on land gave men the idea of making artificial waterways, or canals, especially in the Lowlands. One project for a canal between Glasgow and the Monkland coalfield, had a practical aim: to make coal cheaper in Glasgow, by transporting it cheaply from outside. The other, for a canal across the 'narrow waist' of Scotland between Clyde and Forth, would, it was hoped, encourage trade between west and east, and give Glasgow merchants a direct route to the markets of Europe.

By 1770 work was under way on both canals but shortage of money caused delays in finishing and linking them. The Government helped with £50,000 from the Forfeited Estates (see page 65) and the Forth and Clyde Canal between Grangemouth and Bowling was opened for navigation in 1790. The Monkland Canal was extended to join it in the same year. A further length of canal, the Union, to connect Edinburgh with the Forth and Clyde Canal and therefore with Glasgow, was not completed until 1822, not long before the introduction of railways. It is interesting that many people were attracted to travel on the Forth and Clyde Canal, which had been constructed originally for transporting goods. (See Fig. 2 for these canals):

The Monkland Canal

I have projected a canal to bring coals to the town [Glasgow] for though coal is everywhere hereabouts in plenty, and the very town stands upon it, yet some people have monopolised it and raised its price 50 per cent within these ten years. Now this canal is nine miles long, goes to a country full of level free coals of good quality, in the hands of many proprietors, who sell them at present at sixpence per cart of 7 cwt. at the pit.

James Watt. Letter to Dr. Small, 1769, quoted by E. A. PRATT, *Scottish Canals and Waterways*, p. 145

The Forth and Clyde Canal

Scotland is almost divided into two parts by the rivers Forth and Clyde. These two rivers, falling in opposite directions into the two seas which surround the island, early suggested the idea of cutting the narrow neck of land between them and thereby saving the dangerous navigation by Land's End or the Pentland Firth.

A company was formed and in July 1768, under the direction of Mr. John Smeaton, began to break ground, and the Canal was rendered navigable on 10th July, 1775, as far as Stockingfield, which is the point where the side branch to Glasgow goes off. The Canal remained in this situation until, when the Company obtained an aid from the Government of £50,000, they began to carry the Canal westward from Stockingfield towards the river Clyde. In July 1790 the navigation was opened from sea to sea.

The gross revenues this year (1792) are expected to exceed £14,000.

O.S.A., vol. 5, Appendix, pp. 587–90

The important event of opening the Forth and Clyde navigation from sea to sea was evidenced by the sailing of a barge from the basin of the canal near Glasgow to the River Clyde at Bowling Bay. The voyage, which is upwards of twelve miles, was performed in less than four hours, during which the vessel passed through nineteen locks, descending thereby 156 feet from the summit of the canal into the Clyde. The boat passed along that stupendous bridge, the great aqueduct over the Kelvin, exhibiting to spectators below a vessel navigating seventy feet above their heads.

The extreme length of the navigation from the Forth to the Clyde is 35 miles, and the depth 8 feet throughout. The toll dues payable are 2d per ton for each mile, or 5s 10d for the whole length of the canal.

Scots Magazine, July 1790

By means of the new aqueduct and its locks and basins, Glasgow enjoys a communication with the celebrated canal which joins the Forth and the Clyde. This new cut or canal reaches from the original one till it terminates in a fine new basin near the city, called Port Dundas. Vessels of 96 tons and upward conveniently pass this noble canal and we had the satisfaction of seeing one of considerable burden navigated into port.

I. LETTICE, *Tour, Scots Magazine*, p. 459, 1794

Forth and Clyde Canal	No. of passengers
1812	44,000
1813	64,000
1814	75,000
1815	85,000

The introduction of 'swift' boats for passengers only, made the journey from Glasgow to Falkirk seem short, covering twenty-five miles in 3½ hours. Each boat was pulled by two thoroughbred horses, which were changed every two miles. The fares charged were: 4s cabin class, 2s steerage.

Based on E. A. PRATT, *Scottish Canals and Waterways*, pp. 120–1

1. (a) Who surveyed the Monkland Canal?
   (b) How did the people of Glasgow benefit from it?
2. (a) What were the geographical and commercial arguments in favour of a canal between Forth and Clyde?
   (b) When was this canal finally opened?
   (c) How much would it have cost to carry 5 tons of timber from Grangemouth to Glasgow?

To guide your writing.
1. Imagine you were a Glasgow manufacturer in 1790 and explain why you are using the new canals in place of other forms of transport.
2. Why do you think so many people were travelling by boat after 1812 between Glasgow and Falkirk rather than by road?
3. What was the value of canals to trade and travel in Central Scotland about the year 1820?
4. Why do you think their traffic had declined by 1850?

6· THE HIGHLANDS

The Highland Way of Life

In spite of losses through emigration, population increased in every Highland county between 1755 and 1821 (as the Table at the end of the book shows). The demand for land was intensified, rents rose, new land on hillsides was broken in and potatoes, which gave a big yield from a small area, were grown to try to ward off starvation. More and more people were competing for land on which to carry on the traditional subsistence agriculture.

Highland writers, like Mrs. Grant of Laggan, understood the Highlander's opposition to change and praised his pride in his ancestry and his independent spirit. Travellers like John Leyden, the Border poet, on the other hand, were struck by his poverty:

The Spirit of the Highlander

I should love my father not merely as such, because he was the son of the wise and pious Donald, whose memory the whole parish venerates, and the grandson of the gallant Archibald who was the tallest man in the district, who could throw the putting stone further than any Campbell living, and never held a Christmas without a deer of his own killing, four Fingalian greyhounds at his fireside, and sixteen kinsmen sharing his feast. Shall I not be proud of a father, the son of such fathers, of whose fame he is the living record. What is my case is every other Highlander's.

MRS. GRANT OF LAGGAN, *Letters from the Mountains*, vol. 1, p. 56, 1773

It is not easy for those who live in a country like England, where so many of the lower orders have nothing but what they acquire by the labour of a passing day, and possess no permanent property or share of the agricultural produce of the soil, to appreciate the nature of the spirit of independence in countries where the free cultivators of the soil constitute the major part of the population. It can scarcely be imagined how proud a man feels, however small his property may be, when he has a spot of arable land and pasture stocked with corn, horses and cows. He considers himself an independent person.

DAVID STEWART OF GARTH, *Sketches of the Highlanders*, vol. 1, p. 152

Redundant grass and luxurious heath afford abundance to their cattle, who are never housed in winter. Deer, wild fowl and fish are in great plenty. Salmon crowd their rivers, and shell-fish abound on their rugged coasts. Bread is a foreign luxury to them, they raising little or no corn; a ship comes once or twice a year, and brings them a supply of meal in exchange for butter and cheese.

MRS. GRANT OF LAGGAN, *Letters from the Mountains*, vol. 1, p. 115

Farming

Near Taynish in Argyll, ridges of potatoes appeared on the steepest eminences, and green streaks of corn emerged on the summits of the hills amid clusters of white rocks. Almost every spot of arable land appeared cultivated, even where no plough could possibly be employed. On enquiry we found that the spade was used in tillage where the country is very rocky and irregular.

JOHN LEYDEN, *Tour in the Highlands and Western Islands*, 1800, p. 65

The food of the lower classes in Mull consists mainly of potatoes, in the cultivation of which they are very expert. The young people generally devote themselves to a seafaring life.

JOHN LEYDEN, *Tour in the Highlands and Western Islands*, 1800, p. 35

At dinner they talked of the crooked spade (the *caschrom* in Gaelic) and maintained that it was better than the usual garden spade, and that there was an art in tossing it, by which those used to it could work very easily with it. 'Nay,' said Mr. Johnson, 'it may be useful in land where there are many stones to raise, but it certainly is not a good instrument for good land.'

JAMES BOSWELL, *Journal of a Tour to the Hebrides*, p. 225

We were so remote from markets, we (in the Laird's house) had to depend very much on our own produce for most of the necessaries of life. Our flocks and herds supplied us not only with the chief part of our food, but with fleeces to be woven into clothing, blanketing, and carpets, horn for spoons, leather to be dressed at home for various purposes, hair for the masons (for mixing with plaster). Lint-seed was sown to grow into sheeting, shirting, sacking, etc. We brewed our own beer, made our own bread, made our candles. Nothing was brought from afar but wine, groceries and flour, wheat not ripening well so high above the sea. Yet we lived in luxury, game was so plentiful, the river provided trout and salmon, the garden abounded in common fruits and vegetables, and the poultry-yard was ever well furnished.

ELIZABETH GRANT, *Memoirs of a Highland Lady*, p. 194, 1812

1. What made the Highlander feel proud according to (*a*) Mrs. Grant of Laggan and (*b*) David Stewart of Garth?
2. (*a*) In Mrs. Grant's second account, (*i*) what natural resources made the Highlander well-off and (*ii*) which commodity was scarce?
   (*b*) What crop did John Leyden see growing both near Taynish and in Mull?
   (*c*) What impression do you gain of the number of people in Argyll, including Mull, compared with the amount of arable land available there in 1800?
3. (*a*) What is the Gaelic name for the crooked spade?
   (*b*) Where was it (*i*) useful and (*ii*) less useful, in Dr. Johnson's opinion?
4. (*a*) What evidence does Elizabeth Grant give to show that a laird could provide all the necessities of life for his family?
   (*b*) Which commodities did he import from outside?

Houses

By a *house*, I mean a building with one storey over another; by a *hut*, a dwelling with only one floor. The laird, the tacksman and the minister have commonly houses. Wherever there is a house, the stranger finds a welcome.

The wall of a common hut is always built without mortar by a skilful adaptation of loose stones. Sometimes a double wall of stones is raised and the intermediate space is filled with earth. The air is thus completely excluded. Some walls are, I think, formed of turf. Of the meanest huts, the first room is lighted by the entrance, and the second by the smoke hole. The fire is usually made in the middle.

There are huts, or dwellings, of only one storey, inhabited by gentlemen, which have walls cemented with mortar, glass windows, and boarded floors. Of these, all have chimneys, and some chimneys have grates.

DR. SAMUEL JOHNSON, *Journey to the Western Islands*, p. 152, 1773

The houses of the peasants in Mull are most deplorable. Some of the doors are hardly four feet high and the houses themselves, composed of earthen sods in many instances are scarcely twelve. There is often no other outlet of smoke but at the door, the consequence of which is that the women are more squalid and dirty than the men and their features more disagreeable.

JOHN LEYDEN, Tour in the Highlands and Western Islands, 1800, p. 34

Shielings

We refreshed ourselves at a shieling, or turf-house, and bothay, a dairy house where the Highland shepherds or graziers live during the summer with their herds and flocks, and during that season, make butter and cheese. Their whole furniture consists of a few horn spoons, their milking utensils, a couch formed of sods to lie on, and a rug to cover them; their food oatcakes, butter or cheese. They drink milk, whey and sometimes, by way of indulgence, whisky.

T. PENNANT, A Tour in Scotland, p. 107, 1769

Whisky

The distillation of whisky presents an irresistible temptation to the poorer classes, as the boll of barley, which costs thirty shillings, produces by this process, when the whisky is smuggled, between five and six guineas. This distillation has had the most ruinous effects in increasing the scarcity of grain last year, particularly in Islay and Tiree, where the people have subsisted chiefly on fish and potatoes.

JOHN LEYDEN Tour in the Highlands and Western Islands, 1800, p. 79

The whisky was a bad habit, there was certainly too much of it going. At every house it was offered, at every house it must be tasted or offence would be given, so we were taught to believe. Whisky-drinking was and is the bane of that country; from early morning till late at night it went on. Decent gentlewomen began the day with a dram. In the pantry (of our house) a bottle of whisky was the allowance per day, with bread and cheese in any required quantity, for such messengers or visitors whose errands sent them in that direction. The very poorest cottages could offer whisky; all the men engaged in the wood manufacture drank it in goblets three times a day, yet except at a merry-making we never saw anyone tipsy.

ELIZABETH GRANT, Memoirs of a Highland Lady, pp. 198–9, 1812

The wild glens of the north afforded secure retreats for the working of stills. The proprietor of the only distillery now in Glenlivet recollects seeing two hundred illicit stills at work in Glenlivet alone. Owing to the quality of the water and other causes, the whisky of the Glen became famous – indeed smuggled whisky generally was preferred by customers, on account of its mildness and fine flavour.

D. BREMNER, Industries of Scotland, p. 446

We tasted whisky here at Achanalt in Ross-shire which was pro-
nounced to be of the very best and purest, 'unexcised by Kings'.

ROBERT SOUTHEY, *Journal of a Tour in
Scotland in 1819*, p. 150

Peat

The difficulty of winning their peats, which is the only fuel used here,
renders it necessary (for the bigger farmers) to keep so many servants,
and double the number of horses that would be sufficient for their
ploughing. They are kept almost wholly employed drying and carrying
home their peats from the beginning of June, when the sowing is at an
end, till the latter end of August, when the reaping comes on.

O.S.A., vol. 13, p. 340, Barra

1. What distinction does Dr. Johnson draw between a house and
   a hut?
2. (*a*) What is: a tacksman; a shieling; a grazier; a still?
   (*b*) What is the meaning of: illicit; 'unexcised by Kings'?
3. What materials were used for building most Highland houses,
   or huts, as Dr. Johnson calls them?
4. How did Highland dwellings strike these visitors from the
   south?
5. Why does John Leyden condemn whisky-distilling and Elizabeth
   Grant whisky-drinking?
6. Why was peat a burden to the people in the Highlands and
   Islands?

To guide your writing.
1. Using the sources above, describe the features of what may be
   called the traditional way of life in the Highlands in this period,
   paying attention to homes, food, farming in summer and winter,
   and the work of men and women. (For black cattle in the Highland economy see Chapter 2.)
2. For pupils in the Highlands and Islands:
   (*a*) If you live in a village or know one well, try to reconstruct
   a picture of life there about the year 1800, in words accompanied by drawings or plans. The remains of old buildings
   may still exist, some may still be used as houses or byres or
   outbuildings, and on hillsides, marks of cultivation may still
   be seen. Ask old people about the village in their childhood.
   The *Old Statistical Account* will contain an account of the
   parish.
   (*b*) Check from the population tables at the end how much the

population of your county increased between 1755 and 1821.

Changes in the Highland Way of Life

Although many features of Highland life appeared to be permanent, the period between 1760 and 1820 in fact saw great changes there. When the clans had been military as well as social organisations, extra tenants would have been welcome additions to their fighting strength. By 1760 they were an embarrassment to chiefs as landlords. They stood in the way of change, when estate improvement became the rage in the Highlands following the example of prosperous Lowland lairds. When bigger farms were created, or sheep-farmers came in from the south, small tenants frequently lost their land. Theirs was a tragedy greater than in the Lowlands because sheep-farming could employ far fewer workers than arable farming, and the Highlanders were farther away from alternative work in the new industrial towns. Young men often found a way out by going to sea or joining the army while many families had to move to Lowland towns, or to America. Thomas Telford was the first to start a programme of public works, such as roads, to provide work, and try to keep people in the Highlands:

Forty years ago, a chieftain walked out attended by ten or twelve followers, with their arms rattling. Now the chief has lost his formidable retinue; and the Highlander walks his heath unarmed and defenceless, with the peaceful submission of a French peasant or English cottager.

The abolition of the local jurisdictions, which had for so many ages been exercised by the chiefs, has its evil and good. When the chiefs were men of knowledge and virtue, their jurisdictions were convenient. No long journeys were necessary, and all false pretences were easily detected. The sentence, when it was passed, could not be evaded. Since the regular judges have made their circuits through the whole country, right has been everywhere more wisely and more equally distributed but the complaint is that the magistrates are too few and often too remote for general convenience.

[Stripped of their power] the chiefs turned their thoughts to the improvement of their revenues, and expect more rent. The tenant refuses to pay the demand and is ejected. The ground is then let to a stranger, who perhaps brings in a larger stock. Thus the estate perhaps is improved but the clan is broken.

Among other changes, the use of the bagpipe begins to be forgotten, but I had my dinner exhilarated by the bagpipe at Armidale, Dunvegan, and in Coll.

DR. SAMUEL JOHNSON, *Journey to the Western Islands*, pp. 137, 143–4, 155–6, 1773

The Forfeited Estates

After the '45, the Gentle Lochiel's estate was forfeited and the tenants paid the usual rent to the Crown; besides this they voluntarily paid a rent to support Lochiel's family abroad.

MRS. GRANT OF LAGGAN, *Letters from the Mountains*, vol. 1, p. 106, 1773

The profits of these estates are lodged in the hands of Trustees, who apply their revenue for the founding of schools for the instruction of children in spinning; wheels are given away to poor families, and flax-seed to farmers. Some money is given in aid of the roads and towards building bridges over the torrents, by which means a steady intercourse is made to parts before inaccessible to strangers. The factors, or agents of these estates are also allowed all the money they expend in planting.

T. PENNANT, *A Tour in Scotland*, p. 149, 1769

It is expedient that the said estates be now restored to the heirs or families of the former owners on payment of certain sums on account of the debts due by the forfeiting persons:

To Donald Cameron, son and heir of Charles Cameron, deceased, who was the only lawful son of Donald Cameron, late of Lochiel, the lands, etc. forfeited by the said Donald Cameron, upon paying £3,433 9s 1d.

To Col. Duncan M'Pherson, only lawful son of Evan M'Pherson, late of Cluny, the lands, etc. forfeited by the said Evan M'Pherson, upon paying £5,138 17s 11d,

and to others . . .

The Board of Trustees for Annexed Estates is to be discontinued from Martinmas. The sum of £15,000 of the money paid in is to be given for finishing the office building at Edinburgh for the records of Scotland, and £50,000 towards finishing the canal between Forth and Clyde.

Scots Magazine, vol. 46, pp. 125–7, 1784

The restoration of the forfeited estates [to their former chiefs or their heirs in 1784] has produced no good in the Highlands. Far better would it have been for the country in general, and especially for the poor Highlanders, if the estates had been retained as Crown lands, and leased accordingly, or even sold to strangers. A few of the Highland Lairds are desirous of improving their own estates by bettering the conditions of their tenants. But the greater number are fools at heart: their object is to increase their revenue and they care not by what means this is accomplished. If a man improve his farm, they invite others to out-bid him in the rent; or they dispeople whole tracts to convert them into sheep-farms.

ROBERT SOUTHEY, *Journal of a Tour in Scotland in 1819*, p. 209

1. What were 'local jurisdictions exercised by chiefs'?
2. (a) What had been (i) the advantages and (ii) disadvantages of this system?
   (b) What were (i) the advantages and (ii) disadvantages of the new system?
   (c) How did the abolition of local jurisdiction affect (i) the chief and (ii) the clan?
3. (a) When was the law banning the playing of bagpipes abolished?
   (b) What does Dr. Johnson's account of hearing them suggest about the enforcement of this law?
4. (a) Whose estates were forfeited to the Crown?
   (b) Make a list of the benefits which Pennant says accrued to the Highlands when these estates were administered by Crown Trustees.
   (c) Name two undertakings in the south which benefited from the return of these estates in 1784.
   (d) Why was Robert Southey critical of the restoration of these lands to the families who formerly owned them?

Sheep-farming as a Cause Of Emigration

The most powerful cause of emigration is converting large districts of the country into sheepwalks. This not only requires much fewer people to manage the same tract of country, but in general an entirely new people who have been accustomed to this mode of life, are brought in from the southern parts of Scotland.

The difference of rents to the landlords between sheep and black cattle is, I understand, at least three to one.

In some very few cases a greater population than the land can support in any shape has been the cause of emigrations; such was the island of Tiree.

The people, when turned out of their black-cattle farms to make way for the sheep-farmers, see no mode of employment in their own country, and sooner than seek it in the Lowlands of Scotland or in England, they will believe what is told them may be done in the farming line in America.

THOMAS TELFORD, *1st Report*, 1803

In vain I tried the Highlanders to keep
From being devour'd by flocks of Lowland sheep;
But rage for rent extinguished every thought
For men who bravely had our battles fought.

GEORGE DEMPSTER, *Bragadocio*, 1809, quoted in
Letters to Sir Adam Fergusson, p. 320

The sheep farming system in Glencoe has done the work of extirpation of the inhabitants more effectively than the Massacre of 1692.

W. LARKIN, *A Tour through the Highlands in 1818*, p. 221

Since the month of April last, six vessels have sailed from the Western Islands and other parts of the Highlands, all full of passengers for North Carolina in order to settle in that colony. It is thought that of men, women and children no fewer than 1,200 have embarked in the above ships.

Scots Magazine, p. 457, Aug. 1770

M'Queen said that seventy men had gone out of the Glen [Glenmoriston in Inverness-shire] to America. That he himself intended to go next year; for that the rent of his farm, which twenty years ago was only five pounds, was now raised to twenty pounds. That he could pay ten pounds and live; but no more. Dr. Johnson said he wished M'Queen laird of Glenmoriston, and the laird to go to America.

JAMES BOSWELL, *Journal*, p. 104

We performed a dance which I suppose the emigration from Skye has occasioned. They call it 'America'. The dance seems intended to show how emigration catches, till a whole neighbourhood is set afloat. Mrs. M'Kinnon told me that last year when a ship sailed from Portree for America, the people on shore were almost distracted when they saw their relations go off; they lay down on the ground, tumbled and tore the grass with their teeth. This year there was not a tear shed. The people on shore seemed to think that they would soon follow. This indifference is a mortal sign for the country.

JAMES BOSWELL, *Journal*, p. 245

The Raising of Highland Regiments

Although the Elder Pitt claimed the credit for the policy of enlisting Highlanders in the British army, Duncan Forbes of Culloden had been trying to persuade the Government to take this step long before Pitt came to power. Highland regiments served in the Seven Years War (1756–63) against France, in the War of American Independence (1775–83), and in the French Revolutionary and Napoleonic Wars (1793–1815). The letter of service for the raising of the second battalion of the Seaforth Highlanders in the chapter on Scotsmen and the War against France shows how these regiments were formed:

I sought for merit wherever it was to be found. It is my boast that I was the first minister who looked for it and found it in the mountains of the north. I called it forth and drew into your service a hardy and intrepid race of men. These men in the last war (the Seven Years War) were brought to combat on your side; they served with fidelity as they fought with valour and conquered for you in every part of the world.

Speech of WILLIAM PITT THE ELDER, quoted by
B. WILLIAMS in *The Whig Supremacy*, p. 357

No villages, magazines or harbours were formed, or manufactures introduced, by which the people might be usefully employed; nor hath the smallest ray of hope been held out, whereby they might expect to see better days. On the contrary it seems to be a political maxim with many persons, that the Highlands of Scotland are to be considered merely as a nursery for soldiers and seamen; that the inhabitants, formed admirably by nature for the fatigues of the campaign and the ocean, are to be employed in these capacities alone; and that, to facilitate the business of recruiting, it is necessary to keep them low.

JOHN KNOX, *A View of the British Empire*,
vol. 1, pp. 132–3, 1785

1. (a) What was the main cause of emigration from the Highlands according to Telford, Dempster and Larkin?
   (b) What other cause is mentioned by Telford?
   (c) Why did M'Queen intend to emigrate from Glenmoriston?
   (d) Does Boswell, in the second extract from his *Journal*, suggest a further reason for emigration?
2. (a) Where did most emigrants go in the early 1770's?
   (b) What was the reaction of the people of Portree to the departure of the latest emigrant ship and why?
3. Why did the Elder Pitt boast about his part in raising Highland regiments?
4. (a) How did the Government regard the Highlands, in Knox's view?
   (b) What circumstances made many Highlanders enlist?

To guide your writing.
1. Consider the following changes in this period and try to assess the effects of each on the traditional way of life in the Highlands:
   (a) the abolition of heritable jurisdictions
   (b) estates forfeited to the Crown
   (c) their return to the heirs of former chiefs
   (d) the increase in population
   (e) the creation of sheep farms
2. Analyse the causes of emigration from the Highlands and Islands.
3. You will find *Memoirs of a Highland Lady* by Elizabeth Grant of Rothiemurchus a most readable and fascinating account of her life on an estate in the Cairngorms at this time.

Roads and Canals

Except for trying to repair the military roads, little was done to make travel easier in the Highlands before 1800. Even the maintenance of military roads was becoming difficult to justify as the decay of the clan system reduced the need for a military occupation of the Highlands. These roads, which linked forts with each other and with the Lowlands, were seldom in the best places for ease of movement by people within the region. This was particularly true of the north-west Highlands: although roughly half the Highland area lies north and west of the Great Glen, there were only two military roads there.

Concerned to solve 'the Highland problem', as they saw it – backward agriculture, a low standard of living, increasing population and consequent emigration, reformers gave priority to the improvement of communications. They also saw that it would provide work for local people and Thomas Telford used this argument in his proposals for the improvement of communications and trade in the Highlands in 1803. Telford, the Dumfries-shire stone-mason who became one of the first civil engineers, was already famous for the roads, bridges and canals he had constructed in England. He was to devote so much of his time and boundless energy in the next twenty years to the Highlands that he became almost a one-man Highland Development Board:

Do not forget our Highland roads. In the happy state of our finances, the judicious application of a few thousand on piercing the north and west Highlands with good roads would be a most patriotic application of public money and quickly repay the bountiful Treasury for its expenditure.

Letter of G. Dempster, quoted in *Letters to Sir Adam Fergusson*, 1792, p. 210

From the best information I have been able to procure, about three thousand people went away in the course of the last year and if I am rightly informed three times that number are preparing to leave the country in the present year. If there are any public works to be executed, which when completed will prove generally beneficial to the country, it is advisable these works should be undertaken at the present time. This would furnish employment for the industrious and valuable part of the people in their own country, they would by this means be accustomed to labour, they would acquire some capital and the foundations would be laid for future employments. The Caledonian Canal and roads and bridges are of this description and will not only furnish present employment but promise to accomplish improvements in the future welfare of the country, whether in agriculture, fisheries or manufactures.

THOMAS TELFORD, *1st Report*, 1803

Parliament accepted his Report and undertook to pay the whole cost of the Caledonian Canal and half the cost of all roads and bridges on condition that local landowners put up the other half required. Because of the engineering difficulties and the great distances involved, Parliament was agreeing to help the northern counties to build roads which would have been far beyond the resources of Turnpike Trusts. As the planner, Telford came north every year to inspect and advise, and to gather information for the next stage of the work. He had a gift for choosing reliable and knowledgeable deputies to inspect the work done by contractors. Outstanding among these was John Mitchell, a stone-mason like himself, who became chief inspector. Making allowance for the excessive praise common in such memorials, the inscription quoted below is a fair tribute both to him and the works he supervised:

Every year Telford spent six weeks or two months in going over the canal works and the Highland roads, and my father, John Mitchell, always went with him. They drove in a gig where the roads were made and rode on horseback in other parts.

JOSEPH MITCHELL, *Reminiscences of My Life in the Highlands*, vol. 1, p. 83

Sacred to the Memory
of
JOHN MITCHELL
who died on the 20th Sept. 1824
Principal Inspector
to the Parliamentary Commissioners
for roads and bridges for eighteen years
His eminent skill,
his unwearied activity,
and his honest zeal,
in the superintendence of these great national works,
the roads extending more than 900 miles in length,
the bridges exceeding 1,100 in number
The whole, constructed at an expense of half a million sterling
obtained for him
the constant approbation of his employers
and the general esteem of all who witnessed his official conduct.

JOSEPH MITCHELL, *Reminiscences*, vol. 1, p. 113

1. (a) Who, according to George Dempster, was to pay for improved roads in the Highlands?
   (b) How in fact were they paid for?
2. What argument did Telford use to justify the construction of roads and the Caledonian Canal?

3. Extract the figures for road and bridge construction from the tribute to John Mitchell.

Methods of Road-making

The plan upon which Telford proceeds in roadmaking is this: first to level and drain: then, like the Romans, to lay a solid pavement of large stones, the broad end downwards, as close as they can be set, the points are then broken off, and a layer of stones, broken to about the size of walnuts, laid over them, so that the whole are bound together; over all a little gravel if it be at hand, but this is not essential.

In a country like this [Ross-shire] where there is little use of wheel carriages, the road is constructed wholly of gravel, and all the (big) stones are picked out and thrown aside.

ROBERT SOUTHEY, *Journal of a Tour in Scotland in 1819*, pp. 54 and 149

Tolls

The County of Inverness obtained an act for levying a toll at Lovat Bridge: they have never yet thought it worth while to erect a toll house. At Helmsdale, there is such a house, but the man who rents it never demands toll: the house and the privilege of selling whisky are well worth the rent he pays and he gives up the toll as not worth the trouble of collecting it.

ROBERT SOUTHEY, *Journal*, p. 130

Improvements

The following extracts from the Report of 1821 illustrate the kind of improvements Telford and his men achieved in the Highlands:

BONAR BRIDGE: The Dornoch Firth used to prohibit access to Sutherland and Caithness, unless by means of an inconvenient and dangerous ferry. The heritors of the County of Sutherland resolved to contribute towards throwing a bridge over the firth at Bonar; and this was effected in 1812. It consists of an iron arch, one hundred and fifty feet in span, and two stone arches of sixty and fifty feet respectively. The bridge cost not much less than £14,000, great expense having been incurred in the foundation of its piers and abutments.

ROADS IN SKYE: Full one hundred miles of road have been accomplished, and almost entirely by the hands of the islanders, who have acquired habits of productive industry and skill in the use of more efficient tools.

TOBERMORY PIER: At Tobermory, in the Isle of Mull, the British Fishery Society have an established station, which they were desirous of improving by a landing pier. It extends three hundred feet into the bay, with a head or short return pier. The work was finished in Nov. 1814, within twenty months from the date of the application to us for aid.

Life of Thomas Telford, ed. RICKMAN, Appendix L.3, pp. 399, 385, 409

Opinions on the New Roads

In the Highlands of Scotland where within the memory of man neither a good road nor a good inn were to be found, the roads are now among the best and the inns are now among the most convenient and comfortable in the whole world.

W. LARKIN, *Tour in the Highlands of Scotland in 1818*, p. 24

Someone was praising the good road to Perth to the Duke of Atholl at whose expense it was made, in the presence of Neil Gow, a performer on the violin, of some renown in these parts. Neil replied, 'They may praise your braid roads that gains by 'em; for my part, when I'se gat a wee droppy at Perth, I'se just as lang again in getting hame by the new road as by the auld one.'

ROBERT SOUTHEY, *Journal*, p. 49

1. How did Telford's normal method of building roads differ from that used by Macadam (see page 54).
2. Why were tolls less productive in the Highlands than in the Lowlands?
3. Who would benefit from the construction of (*a*) Bonar Bridge (*b*) roads in Skye (*c*) Tobermory Pier?

Canals

Highland areas are seldom suitable for canal construction, but two routes commended themselves, one across the neck of Kintyre, and the other cleaving through the heart of the Highlands by linking up the lochs in the Great Glen:

THE CRINAN CANAL: A voyage between the Atlantic and the Clyde, which frequently takes up three weeks, would by this easy passage be performed in three or four days, in all seasons of the year. By cutting off the peninsula of Kintyre, the voyage would be entirely inland and

PLATE 8. Early nineteenth-century leisure and dress. *Top left:* Alexander McKellar, a keen golfer who devoted every moment of his leisure time to the sport. *Top right:* H. E. Johnston, a well known actor of the period, in the role of *Hamlet. Above left:* An oyster seller in picturesque garb. *Above right:* Two 'Tron men' or chimney sweeps.

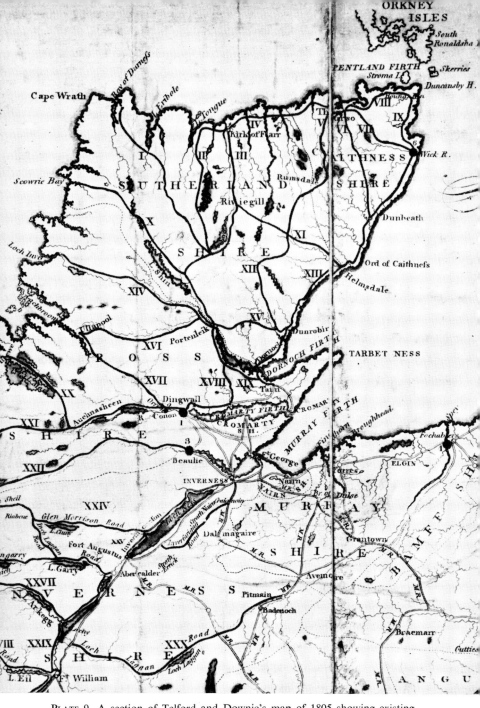

PLATE 9. A section of Telford and Downie's map of 1805 showing existing and proposed bridges (the large black dots) and roads in the Highlands. (See pp. 49, 69–72.)

thereby screened in great measure from the dreadful tempests of the Atlantic.

JOHN KNOX, *View of the British Empire*,
vol. 2, p. 416, 1785, 3rd Edition

The canal was surveyed by John Rennie in 1792 and completed in 1801. John Leyden visited it in 1800:

A considerable part of the Crinan Canal is still unfinished. The locks to be employed are about fifteen in number and their breadth is twenty-seven feet. The depth of the canal is about twelve and a half feet. About 800 or 900 people have been frequently employed upon it, though at present there are not above 300. It has already cost about £110,000 and will require about £10,000 more. It will probably be finished in another year.

JOHN LEYDEN, *Tour in the Highlands and Western Islands*, p. 61

1. Find the Crinan Canal on the map (Fig. 2) and see if you would have supported John Knox's view of its usefulness.
2. Who was the engineer responsible for it?

THE CALEDONIAN CANAL: This Canal through the Great Glen, on the other hand, was the work of Telford. Much earlier, it had been foreseen by the most famous Highlander with the gift of prophecy, the seventeenth-century Brahan Seer, but such a project seemed difficult and dangerous to Captain Burt, an engineer with General Wade in the Highlands in the 1720's and '30's:

Strange as it may seem to you this day, the time will come, and it is not far off, when full-rigged ships will be seen sailing eastward and westward by the back of Tomnahurich [inland] at Inverness.

Prophecies of the BRAHAN SEER, ed. A. MACKENZIE, p. 9

It would be an incredible expense to cut fourteen navigable miles in so rocky a country and there is yet a stronger objection. The whole opening lies in so direct a line, and the mountains that bound it are so high, the wind is confined in its passage, as it were in the nozzle of a pair of bellows; so that let it blow from whatever quarter it will without [i.e. outside] the opening, it never varies much from east or west within.

This would render the navigation so precarious that hardly anybody would venture on it.

BURT, *Letters*, vol. 2, pp. 211–12

Telford recommended that the Canal be constructed, believing that it

D

would be of great value to shipping when it was completed. He was also confident that it would help to train the Highlanders in the routine of regular work but as the years passed his opinion changed. The Highlanders' preference for seasonal work, because of other interests such as fishing and peat-cutting, was only one of his many difficulties:

The people have already fallen into the necessary modes of employment and will soon acquire habits of industry which will prove a lasting benefit to themselves, improve that part of the United Kingdom and put a final stop to the spirit of emigration.

THOMAS TELFORD, *1st Canal Report*, 1804

The herring season has been most abundant, and the return of the fine weather will enable the indolent Highland creatures to get their plentiful crops and have a glorious spell at the whisky-making.

Telford's Letter Sept. 1818, quoted by A. R. B. HALDANE, in *New Ways through the Glens*, p. 83

Rising Wages	1803-5	1812
Labourers	1s 6d – 2s	3s – 3s 6d
Carpenters	2s 3d – 2s 6d	2s 10d – 3s 4d
Masons	2s 8d	3s 6d
Blacksmiths	2s 6d – 3s	3s 6d – 4s

Life of Telford, ed. RICKMAN, p. 310

Life and Work of the canal-builders

Men, horses and machines were at work, making a lock at Fort Augustus: digging, walling and puddling going on, men wheeling barrows, horses drawing stones along the railways. The great engine was at rest, having done its work. It threw out 160 hogsheads per minute (a hogshead is 52½ gallons). The dredging machine was in action, revolving round and round, and bringing up at every turn matter which had never before been brought to the air and light. Its chimney poured forth volumes of black smoke.

ROBERT SOUTHEY, *Journal*, p. 184

I accompanied the workmen for four months to a lock that was in course of construction at Kyllachy, close to Loch Oich, about six miles from Fort Augustus. I lodged with about thirty masons in a house built for the lock-keeper. The men slept in temporary beds, one above the other, like the berths on a ship. The men began work at 6 a.m., one being told off to cook about half an hour before meals. The breakfast was at nine o'clock, the fare consisting of porridge and milk and thick oaten bannocks. They dined at two on the same fare, and at eight had supper.

The fare varied when the new potatoes came in and fresh herrings were brought down from Loch Hourn in the autumn. On Sundays they luxuriated in tea, oaten bannocks and butter for breakfast.

Sunday was reverently kept. The men were perfectly sober, never tasting spirits or beer, and as the cost of living amounted only to 3s 6d or 4s a week out of wages of 21s each had a very considerable sum to bring home to his wife and family.

The Highlanders who were labourers lived chiefly on brose, i.e. meal in a bowl, a little salt, and hot water mixed into a mess. There was little or no drinking with them here for there was no public house within three miles of the place; but at Fort Augustus after a pay-day, which was once a month, they took to drinking and quarrelling, and spent then as much money as would have fed them comfortably the whole month.

JOSEPH MITCHELL, Reminiscences of My Life in the Highlands, vol. I, pp. 81–2

Ceremonial Opening

Charles Grant, late M.P. for Inverness-shire said in his speech: 'It will not only open a direct inland communication by water between the eastern and western coasts of Britain, but also avoid the stormy and circuitous navigation of the Pentland Firth and Cape Wrath, thus enabling ships, British and Irish, in the Baltic trade to pass at once through a safe inland channel to the northern countries of Europe. In times of emergency frigates of war may also pass by the same channel from the west of Britain to the North Sea.'

Then [on Wednesday, 24th October, 1822] the voyagers departed in a small steam yacht from Muirtown Locks, Inverness, with fine weather and high spirits. As they passed, groups from the glens and braes were stationed to behold the welcome pageant and add their lively cheers to the thunder of the guns and the music of the Inverness-shire militia band.

On Thursday at last they reached Banavie where eight grand locks, close to each other, have been fancifully called 'Neptune's Staircase'. Three hours were occupied in passing through these locks and the three others near the sea, so that it was half-past five o'clock when the vessel at last dipped her keel into the waters of the Western Ocean amid the loud acclamations of her passengers and a great concourse of spectators!

Inverness Courier, 31 Oct., 1822

Tribute by Robert Southey, the Poet Laureate, engraved on a tablet at the Caledonian Canal Office, Inverness:

> Telford it was by whose presiding mind
> The whole great work was planned and perfected;
> Telford, who o'er the vale of Cambrian Dee

Aloft in air at giddy height upborne
Carried his navigable road; and hung
High o'er Menai's Strait the bending bridge: . . .
Nor hath he for his native land performed
Less in this proud design: and where his piers
Around her coast from many a fisher's creek
Unsheltered else, and many an ample port
Repel the assailing storm: and where his roads
In beautiful and sinuous line far seen
Wind with the vale and win the long ascent
Now o'er the deep morass sustained, and now
Across ravine, or glen or estuary
Opening a passage through the wilds subdued.

1. What fears did Captain Burt have about a canal through the Great Glen?
2. Why was Telford in favour of it?
3. What benefits did Charles Grant think the Canal would bring?
4. For what reasons did the Highland labourers appear to be less reliable workers than the masons with whom Joseph Mitchell lived and worked?
5. What was the function of (a) the great engine and (b) the dredging machine in Southey's description of work on the Canal?
6. Southey's lines in his tribute to Telford are much more than a collection of beautiful phrases skilfully strung together, for on examination they tell a great deal about Telford's works in Scotland and elsewhere. Study them and see if you can explain:
   (a) what he means by: a 'navigable road'; 'the bending bridge'; 'wind with the vale and win the long ascent',
   (b) what two achievements by Telford are mentioned in lines 3–6 of the poem,
   (c) what the poet tells us about Telford's works in the Highlands.

To guide your writing.
1. Why did the Highlands require special treatment with regard to roads and canals compared with the Lowlands?
2. How would life, work, trade and knowledge in the Highlands benefit from improved communications?
3. (a) Why did the Caledonian Canal cost more than was expected?
   (b) Why do you think it proved less useful than expected?
4. As a mason on the Canal near Fort Augustus who had previously worked with Telford in England, record your impressions of the work, your workmates and your surroundings.
5. Making use of the map in Plate 9 and the sources quoted here, write your own account of Telford's achievements in the Highlands.

6. In Rennie, Macadam and Telford, Scotland produced three outstanding early civil engineers. See what else you can find out
   about each of them.

The Sutherland Clearances

The county of Sutherland was remote and undeveloped, a rough wasteland of mountain and moor encircling tiny patches of cultivation, where
poor but hardy people scraped a living from unfriendly soil. Between
1812 and 1819, thousands of people were moved from their holdings
there to make room for sheep. A map of the Strathnaver Clearance is on
page 91.

Few topics in Scottish history have aroused more controversy among
historians than these Sutherland Clearances. Three accounts of the
eviction of tenants from Strathnaver in 1819 are given here by writers
who knew Sutherland at the time. The first is by James Loch, a lawyer
from the south, who became Commissioner of the Sutherland estates.
He planned to improve the lands under his control, by creating large
sheep farms and removing the tenants to the north coast. He wrote as
'the landlord's man' and his point of view is clear enough:

The men being impatient of regular and constant work, all the heavy
labour was abandoned to the women, who were employed, occasionally,
even in dragging the harrow to cover the seed. To build their hut, or
get in their peats for fuel, the men were ever ready to assist; but most
of their time, when not in pursuit of game, or illegal distillation, was
spent in indolence and sloth. They were contented with the most simple
and the poorest fare. They deemed no comfort worth the possession
which was to be purchased at the price of regular work. The cattle which
they reared on the mountains, and from the sale of which they depended
for the payment of their rents, were of the poorest description.

The coast of Sutherland abounds with many different kinds of fish,
not only sufficient for the consumption of the country but affording a
supply for more distant markets, when cured and salted. It seemed as
if it had been pointed out by Nature that the system for this remote
district was to convert the mountainous districts into sheep-walks, and
to remove the inhabitants to the coast.

The people who were to be removed were to hold their farms, during
the last year of their occupation, rent-free on condition of their settling
in their new lots without delay; and it was ordered that the moss fir
belonging to their huts should be purchased from them because it would
have been impossible for them to have carried it off. Some of the people,
however, reappeared and constructed new, or repaired their old turf
huts, and reoccupied their former possessions. This rendered a second

ejectment necessary and, to prevent the possibility of its repetition, the only course which could be pursued was to collect and burn the timber. This simple and necessary act has been falsified in every possible way. The most positive and direct denial is given to every account in which it has been attempted to apply to these proceedings the character of cruelty and oppression.

The whole of the population from Altnaharra to Invernaver have been settled on the sea shore, as near to the various creeks as it is possible to arrange. These people have begun to cultivate their lots with much industry. Many of them have with great boldness taken to catch cod and ling. They have become as expert boatmen as any in the world.

JAMES LOCH, *An Account of the Improvements of the Estates of the Marquess of Stafford in Sutherland*, 1820, pp. 51, 63–4, 86, 99–100

1. (*a*) What is James Loch's opinion of the men of Sutherland:
     (*i*) before they were moved from the hills,
     (*ii*) after they had settled on the coast?
   (*b*) Do you think the move to the coast changed the men's attitude to work, or do you think Loch's views contradict one another?
2. (*a*) Why did he want the people to move?
   (*b*) Did the people want to go?
3. What is his explanation of 'the burning'?

Rev. Donald Sage was the missionary at Achness, across Loch Naver from Grummore. Even at this time when ministers were appointed to parishes by landlords, Donald Sage's sympathy lay with the people when they had to leave their homes:

To my poor and defenceless flock the dark hour of trial came in right earnest. It was in the month of April 1819 that they were all – man, woman and child – from the Heights of Farr to the mouth of the Naver, on one day to quit their tenements and go – many of them knew not whither. For a few, some miserable patches of ground along the shore were doled as lots without anything in the shape of the poorest hut to shelter them. Upon these lots it was decided that they should build houses at their own expense, and cultivate the ground, at the same time occupying themselves as fishermen, although the great majority of them had never set foot in a boat in their lives.

At an early hour on a Tuesday, Mr. Sellar, escorted by a large body of constables, sheriff-officers and others, commenced work at Grummore, the first inhabited township to the west. They gave the inmates half an hour to pack up and carry off their furniture and then set the cottages on fire. To this plan they ruthlessly adhered. The roofs and rafters were lighted up into one red blaze.

I had occasion the next week to visit the manse of Tongue. On my way thither, I passed through the scene of the campaign of burning. Of all the houses, the thatched roofs were gone; but the walls remained. The flames of the preceding week still slumbered in their ruins, and sent up into the air spiral columns of smoke. The sooty rafters of the cottages as they were being consumed, filled the air with a heavy and most offensive odour. Nothing could more vividly represent the horrors of grinding oppression.

DONALD SAGE, *Memorabilia Domestica*, p. 215

1. What is Donald Sage's opinion of:
   (*a*) the notice given to the Strathnaver people to quit,
   (*b*) the way in which they were cleared out?
2. What does he think of:
   (*a*) the lands given to them on the coast,
   (*b*) their prospects as fishermen?
3. How does he explain 'the burning'?

Donald Macleod was a stone-mason from Rossal in Strathnaver. He and his family had suffered eviction earlier and he saw what happened in the clearance of 1819. His book *Gloomy Memories* was widely read and became the commonly accepted view of the Sutherland Clearances. His critics maintain that his account is exaggerated because it was not published until twenty years after the events he described and because he wrote with anger against the landlord because of his own eviction:

I was an eye-witness of the scene. This calamity came on the people quite unexpectedly. Strong parties, for each district, furnished with faggots and other combustibles, rushed on the dwellings of this devoted people, and immediately commenced setting fire to them, proceeding in their work with the greatest rapidity till about three hundred houses were in flames! The consternation and confusion were extreme; little or no time was given for the removal of persons or property – the people striving to remove the sick and the helpless before the fire should reach them – next, struggling to save the most valuable of their effects. The cries of the women and children – the roaring of the affrighted cattle hunted at the same time by the yelling dogs of the shepherds amid the smoke and fire – altogether presented a scene that completely baffles description: it required to be seen to be believed.

A dense cloud of smoke enveloped the whole country by day and even extended far on the sea; at night an awfully grand but terrific scene presented itself – all the houses in an extensive district in flames at once! I myself ascended a height about eleven o'clock in the evening, and counted two hundred and fifty blazing houses, many of the owners of which were my relations, and all of whom I personally knew; but whose present condition, whether in or out of the flames, I could not tell. The conflagration lasted six days, till the whole of the dwellings were reduced to ashes or smoking ruins.

DONALD MACLEOD, *Gloomy Memories*, pp. 16–17, 1892

1. How many houses does Donald Macleod say were on fire (*a*) at first and (*b*) at night?
2. How does he explain 'the burning'?

To guide your writing.
1. Study these three accounts carefully and note the occasions on which one version confirms the information given in another. Then consider whether any version refutes statements in another and whether it does so convincingly. When you have done this, some of the facts will appear to be reasonably reliable while about others there may be some doubt or difference of opinion.
   As if you were a reporter who knew Sutherland in 1819 write your own account, paying attention to (*a*) the motives of the landowner, (*b*) what was provided for the people on the coast, (*c*) the methods adopted to persuade them to go there and (*d*) the viewpoints of the writers you are using as sources.
2. Two interesting modern books about the Sutherland Clearances are *The Trial of Patrick Sellar*, by Ian Grimble and *The Highland Clearances*, by John Prebble. Read as much as you can and see whether you change your opinions from what you wrote in answer to Question 1.

7 · CHANGING CITIES

Edinburgh

During the reign of George III both Edinburgh and Glasgow grew in population and area and importance. No longer a political capital, Edinburgh continued to be a centre for education, law and business and still attracted many of the nobility and gentry who had town houses there. It also became the haunt of literary men, some Edinburgh-born, some connected with the University, and some who came from outside, like Robert Burns, when the Kilmarnock edition of his poems suddenly made him known. Their presence and their publications gave Edinburgh a new claim to fame as a cultural capital. At the same time, the city burst out of its medieval shape. With the erection of the North Bridge, it expanded to the north side of the Nor' Loch, according to architect James Craig's plan for the New Town.

The Old Town

The principal or great street runs along the ridge of a very high hill, which, taking its rise from the palace of Holyrood House, ascends and not very gradually, for the length of a mile and a quarter, and after opening a spacious area, terminates in the Castle.

The style of building here is much like the French: the houses, however, in general are higher and some run to twelve stories in height. This mode of dwelling has now lost its convenience. As they no longer stand in need of the defence from the Castle, they no more find the benefit of being crowded together so near it. The common staircase which leads to the apartments of the different inhabitants, must always be dirty, and is in general very dark and narrow.

E. TOPHAM, *Letters from Edinburgh*, pp. 8–9

Dr. Johnson and I walked arm in arm up the High Street. As we marched along he acknowledged that the breadth of the street and the loftiness of the buildings on each side made a noble appearance.

JAMES BOSWELL, *Journal of a Tour to the Hebrides*, pp. 11–12

I can imagine a visitor going to tea at Mr. Bruce of Kennet's, in Forrester's Wynd – a country gentleman and a lawyer, yet happy to live

81

with his wife and children in a house of fifteen pounds of rent, in a region of profound darkness and mystery now no more. They had just three rooms and a kitchen; one room, 'my lady's' – that is, a kind of parlour; another, a consulting room for the gentleman; the third, a bedroom. The children, with their maid, had beds laid down for them at night in their father's room; the housemaid slept under the kitchen dresser; and the one man-servant was turned at night out of the house.

R. CHAMBERS, *Traditions of Edinburgh*, p. 3 (1967 edition)

The town was, nevertheless, a funny, familiar, compact and not unlikeable place. Gentle and simple living within the compass of a single close, or even a single stair, knew and took an interest in each other. Every forenoon, for several hours, the only clear space which the town presented – that around the Cross – was crowded with loungers of all ranks. Gentlemen and ladies paraded along in the stately attire of the period; tradesmen chatted in groups at their front doors; caddies whisked about, bearing messages or attending to the affairs of strangers; children filled the kennel with their noisy sports. Add to all this, corduroyed men from Gilmerton, bawling coals or yellow sand; fishwomen calling their caller haddies from Newhaven; sootymen with their bags; town-guardsmen with their antique Lochaber axes; water-carriers with their dripping barrels; barbers with their hairdressing materials; and so forth – it was a unique scene, and one which was not easily to be forgotten.

R. CHAMBERS, *Traditions of Edinburgh*, pp. 3–4 (1967 edition)

The New Town

'Look at these fields,' said Provost Drummond. 'You, Mr. Somerville are a young man, and may probably live, though I will not, to see all these fields covered with houses, forming a splendid and magnificent city. To the accomplishment of this nothing is more necessary than draining the Nor' Loch and providing a proper access from the old town. I have never lost sight of this object since the year 1725 when I first became provost.'

THOMAS SOMERVILLE, *My Own Life and Times*, pp. 47–48

From the right of the High Street, you pass over a very long bridge to the New Town, which has been built upon one uniform plan, the only means of making a town beautiful. The rent of the houses in general amount to £100 per annum and upwards, and are most of them let to the inhabitants by the builders. The greatest part of the New Town is built after the manner of the English and the houses are what they call here 'houses to themselves'.

E. TOPHAM, *Letters from Edinburgh*, pp. 11–12

(In designing the New Town) we were led into the blunder of long straight lines of street, divided to an inch by rectangular intersections, every house being an exact duplicate of its neighbour, with an avoidance of every ornament by which the slightest break might vary the surface.

LORD COCKBURN, *Memorials of His Time*, p. 173

In 1763 Edinburgh was almost entirely confined within the city walls. The suburbs were of small extent. To the north, there was no bridge. Now in the 1790's it may with truth be said that there is not now in Europe a more beautiful terrace than Prince's Street, nor a more elegant street than George Street.

In 1763 people of quality and fashion lived in houses (in the Old Town) which, in 1783, were inhabited by tradesmen, or by people in humble and ordinary life. The Lord Justice Clerk's house was possessed by a French teacher, the Lord President's by a rouping-wife or saleswoman of old furniture.

In 1751 the rents of houses liable to land tax within the city were £31,497.

In 1783 the rents of houses liable to land tax within the city were £54,371.

In 1792 the rents of houses liable to land tax within the city were £68,997.

O.S.A., vol. 6, pp. 582–5, Appendix by W. CREECH,
Bookseller, Edinburgh

My father had taken the most disagreeable house possible (in the New Town); a large gloomy No. 11 in Queen Street, on the front of which the sun never shone, and which was so built against behind that there was no free circulation of air through it. It was comfortable within, plenty of rooms in it, four good ones on a floor.

Two years later we removed to Charlotte Square, a house I found the most agreeable of any we had ever lived in in Edinburgh; a peep from the upper windows at the back, of the Firth of Forth with its wooded shores and distant hills, made the outlook so cheerful. We were in the midst, too, of our friends. We made two new acquaintances, the Wolfe Murrays next door, and Sir James and Lady Henrietta Ferguson. Nothing could be pleasanter than our sociable life. Every day some meeting took place between us young people. My mother's tea-table was, I think, the general gathering point. In the mornings we made walking parties, and one day we went to Rosslyn and Lasswade, a merry company.

ELIZABETH GRANT, *Memoirs of a Highland Lady*,
pp. 302, 316, 1815–17

1. What had been the original purpose of building houses closely together in Old Edinburgh?

2. Name the important building at each end of the principal street.
3. (a) How many rooms did Mr. Bruce's house contain?
   (b) Did he think it big enough for his family and servants?
4. (a) Look up any words you do not understand in Chambers's account of life in the Old Town.
   (b) Does he give the impression that people of different social classes in the Old Town kept their distance or inter-mingled with one another?
5. Whose dream was it to create the New Town of Edinburgh?
6. (a) According to Topham, what gave the New Town merit?
   (b) Why did Lord Cockburn criticise it?
7. (a) What evidence is there to show that it was only the well-to-do who moved to the New Town?
   (b) What kind of people moved into the houses they left in the Old Town?
   (c) What effect did the building of the New Town have on the contact between different social classes?

Edinburgh as a Commercial Centre

The most considerable branch of its trade is that retail trade which it possesses as the seat of fashion, and the commercial centre of intercourse for Scotland. Hence those splendid shops which line its streets. Hence is it, that many of its richest and most respected citizens are simply shop-keepers. What vast quantities of cottons, of linens, of silks, of woollen stuffs are retailed here. What abundance of liquors and of grocery goods of all kinds. The cabinetmaker earns very large sums. The tailor is among the most considerable gainers. The materials for the retail trade are sup-plied by a very large importation. From the circumjacent country are brought grain, whisky, sheep, beeves, swine, poultry, wildfowl, fish, cheese, butter, milk, eggs, and indeed all articles of fresh provisions. From England come an innumerable variety of articles, partly its raw produce, partly of its manufactures, and in part imported by the English from Foreign Countries. Happily we can now provide muslins for our own use. But a large quantity of Irish linens are still annually imported into Edinburgh. From France, many articles of the consumpt of our metro-polis have till very lately been directly imported. Timber, iron, leather and coarse linens are brought hither from Russia. From the countries on the Mediterranean, too, are large imports brought into the port of Leith. For our West Indies goods, we begin to be less dependent, than we once were on Glasgow and on London.

R. HERON, *Journey through Scotland*, 1792, vol. 2, pp. 488–9

1. What is meant by: retail trade; metropolis; muslins?
2. How were shop-keepers regarded in Edinburgh?

3. Where did the food of the city come from?
4. What events in France had probably reduced her exports to Edinburgh?

Men of genius

Really it is admirable how many men of genius this country produces at present. Is it not strange that, at a time when we have lost our Princes, our Parliaments, our independent Government, even the presence of our chief Nobility, are unhappy in our accent and pronounciation, speak a very corrupt dialect of the Tongue which we make use of; is it not strange, in these circumstances that we should really be the people most distinguished for literature in Europe?

David Hume to Gilbert Elliot, 1757
Letters of David Hume, vol. II, letter 135, ed. GREIG

In 1763 literary property, or authors acquiring money by their writings was hardly known in Scotland: David Hume and Dr. Robertson had indeed sold some of their works, the one a part of the *History of Britain* for £200; the other, the *History of Scotland* for £600; each two volumes.

In 1783 the value of literary property was carried higher by the Scots than ever was known among any people. David Hume received £5,000 for the remainder of his *History of Britain*; and Dr. Robertson, for his second work received £4,500. The Scots have distinguished themselves in many departments of literature: and within the last twenty years, David Hume, Dr. William Robertson, Adam Smith, Henry Mackenzie, James Macpherson and many others have appeared.

O.S.A., vol. 6, pp. 587–9. Appendix by W. CREECH,
Bookseller, Edinburgh

ROBERT BURNS IN EDINBURGH: Following the success of the Kilmarnock edition, Burns travelled to Edinburgh to win support for a further publication of his poems. The Caledonian Hunt agreed to subscribe and this edition was dedicated to them:

Present	Lord Elibank, Preses
The Duke of Gordon	The Earl of Glencairn
Lord Maitland	Lord Haddo
and nineteen others	

A motion being made by the Earl of Glencairn, and seconded by Sir John Whitefoord, in favour of Mr. Burns of Ayrshire, who had dedicated the new edition of his Poems to the Caledonian Hunt – The meeting were of opinion that, in consideration of his superior merit, as well as the compliment paid to them, Mr. Hagart should be instructed to subscribe for One Hundred copies, in their name, for which he should pay Mr. Burns, Twenty-five-pounds, upon the publication of his book.

Minutes of the Royal Caledonian Hunt, Edinburgh, 10th January, 1787

His eye alone, I think, indicated the poetical character and temperament. It glowed (I say literally *glowed*) when he spoke with feeling or interest. I never saw such another eye in a human head, though I have seen the most distinguished men of my time. Among the men who were the most learned of their time and country he expressed himself with perfect firmness, but without the least forwardness; and when he differed in opinion, he did not hesitate to express it firmly, yet, at the same time, with modesty. He was much caressed in Edinburgh, but the efforts made for his relief were extremely trifling.

Sir Walter Scott, Letter to J. G. Lockhart, quoted by ALLAN CUNNING- HAM, *The Complete Works of Robert Burns*, vol. 1, p. 45

SIR WALTER SCOTT: A genius now appeared, who has immortalised Edinburgh and will long delight the world. In 1805 Walter Scott revealed his true self by the publication of the *Lay of the Last Minstrel*. Nobody, not even Scott, anticipated what was to follow. Nobody imagined the career that was before him, yet his advances were like the conquests of Napoleon: each new achievement overshadowing the last.

LORD COCKBURN, *Memorials of His Time*, pp. 125–6

Waverley came out, I think it must have been in the autumn of 1814. I did not like it. Then burst out *Guy Mannering*, carrying all the world before it. People now began to feel these works could come but from one author, particularly as a few acres began to be added to the recent purchase of the old tower of Abbotsford, and Mrs. Scott set up a carriage built in London, which from the time she got it she was seldom out of.

ELIZABETH GRANT, *Memoirs of a Highland Lady*, p. 326

The unexpected newness of the thing (the novel, *Waverley*), the profusion of original characters, the Scotch language, Scotch scenery, Scotch men and women, the simplicity of the writing, and the graphic force of the descriptions – all struck us with a shock of delight.

LORD COCKBURN, *Memorials of His Time*, p. 168

1. What circumstances made David Hume express surprise that Edinburgh should contain so many 'men of genius'?
2. (*a*) What was the purpose of Burns's visit to Edinburgh?
   (*b*) What was Sir Walter Scott's opinion of (*i*) the poet as a man and (*ii*) the way Edinburgh treated him?

3. (a) Why did people begin to suspect that Sir Walter Scott was the author of *Waverley*?

   (b) Why, in Lord Cockburn's opinion, did people like *Waverley*?

To guide your writing.

1. If you live in Edinburgh, study the Old Town and the New Town for yourself and comment on their merits and defects from the point of view of architecture, street-layout, comfort and social life at that time.

2. Write an account of the expansion of Edinburgh in the reign of George III.

3. Try to find out more about at least three of the writers listed in the extract by Creech and then write an account of Scotland's contribution to literature in the age of Burns and Scott.

4. In what ways could Edinburgh claim to be the capital of Scotland then?

Glasgow

The growth of Glasgow was even more rapid and impressive. After the Union, access to the tobacco trade with the American colonies brought great wealth to the city and Glasgow flourished until the War of American Independence began in 1775 and imports of tobacco practically ceased. Glasgow merchants continued to trade across the Atlantic, bringing in sugar and raw cotton from the West Indies. The city developed as the centre of cotton manufacture and engineering and was soon the capital of industrial Scotland, as heavy industries and ship-building developed along the Clyde:

The Rise in Population

1708 – 12,766	1801 – 83,769
1740 – 17,034	1811 – 116,380
1763 – 28,300	1821 – 147,043
1780 – 42,832	1831 – 202,424
1791 – 66,578	

JAMES PAGAN, *Sketch of the History of Glasgow*, p. 101, 1847

Tobacco Traders

The opportunity to trade with the colonies in America was seized by merchants in Glasgow after the Union. Soon many merchants became very rich, especially by importing tobacco and re-exporting much of it to countries in Europe, which were not permitted then to trade directly with British colonies:

	Imports of tobacco		Re-exports of tobacco	
	lbs.	value	lbs.	value
1755	15,200,698	£158,341	10,477,024	£218,271
1775	45,863,154	£477,741	30,228,949	£629,769
1777	294,896	£3,072	5,406,668	£112,639
1795	2,731,091	£28,348	1,003,268	£20,907

In the year 1771 when imports of tobacco from America were as high as 47,269,000 lbs. re-exports from Scotland totalled over 45 million lbs. to markets in Europe, especially the following:

Denmark and Norway:	1,164,428 lbs.
Germany:	3,873,027 lbs.
Holland	14,932,537 lbs.
Ireland:	3,710,803 lbs.
France:	16,955,232 lbs.

Based on H. HAMILTON, *Economic History of Scotland in the Eighteenth Century.* (Appendices IX and X, pp. 416–18)

I remember our Tobacco lords with their bushy wigs and scarlet cloaks perambulating the plane stanes at the Cross, and keeping other classes at a respectful distance. It was with no little admiration that I beheld the powdered flunkeys of these lords, dressed in plush breeches, with thread stockings, dashing shoe buckles (which covered the whole front of their feet) and with massy brass buttons on their coats, and gold bands on their hats.

R. REID, *Glasgow Past and Present*

In Glasgow I conversed with one Mr. Glassford, whom I take to be one of the greatest merchants in Europe. In the last war (the Seven Years War) he is said to have had at one time five and twenty ships with their cargoes, his own property, and to have traded for half a million (pounds) sterling a year.

TOBIAS SMOLLETT, *Humphrey Clinker* [Fiction], 1771

1. From the population figures for Glasgow:
   (a) find out which decade (period of ten years) showed the greatest increase.
   (b) see how the increase between 1791 and 1821 compares with that between 1763 and 1791.

PLATE 10. Thomas Telford.

PLATE 11. This early nineteenth-century print by Geikie shows the Cowgate, Edinburgh near the foot of Libberton Wynd. Note the stalls and shops.

PLATE 12. Edinburgh's New Town: St. Andrew Square from a print by Shepherd. Compare it with Plate 11.

NUMBER XXXVII.

CITY of GLASGOW,

(COUNTY OF LANARK.)

From the Communications of several respectable Inhabitants of that City.

I.

INTRODUCTORY OBSERVATIONS.

IT cannot be expected, in a work of this kind, that a complete history of this city should be given. It is therefore only intended, to give a concise view of various particulars, tending to illustrate its ancient and present state; referring those, who wish to have a fuller account of its rise and progress, its public buildings, &c. to the histories of it already published, by M'Ure and Gibson.

takes its rise about 50 miles nearer the head of the shire. Its latitude 55° 51′ 32″ north, and its longitude 4° 15′ west from London. A very accurate map of the city was published some years ago, by Mr M'Arthur, and a map of the royalty, under the inspection of the Magistrates, by the town's surveyor. It is proposed to publish a map of its environs for 7 miles.—The tide flows, (at least at spring tides,) nearly about 4 miles above the city; but he Clyde, until of late years, was only navigable to Glasgow by small vessels, and even these met with many obstructions from the numerous shoals and sand banks which were in it. This inconvenience was much felt by the inhabitants, and many proposals were made to have it remedied. As far back as the reign of Queen Mary, it is reported, that many hundreds of the citizens of Glasgow, in conjunction with the inhabitants of Renfrew and Dumbarton, under the inspection of officers appointed by the Magistrates, lived for six weeks, *per vices,* in tents and huts, about 13 miles below Glasgow, endeavouring to remove the obstruction of the river at Dumbuck Ford. These, or similar efforts, however, had not the desired effect; and hence, after several surveys, an act of Parliament was obtained in 1759, in order to render it navigable for large vessels, by means of locks. Many difficulties, however, having occurred, this scheme was dropped, and another act was afterwards obtained, for improving the navigation of the river, from Dumbuck Ford to Glasgow, by deepening the bed of the river, and straitening the channel by means of jetties on the sides of it; for defraying the expence of which, a tonnage duty of 8 d. a-ton on coals, and 1 s. a-ton on all goods and merchandize, that should be carried be-

PLATE 13. A page from Sir John Sinclair's *Statistical Account of Scotland.*

PLATE 14. Cartoonist John Kay makes fun of the indecision of Edinburgh Councillors. While the Lord Provost attempts to level the High Street, an opponent fills in the hole. In the foreground, three other councillors discuss the plan.

PLATE 15. Adam Smith.

PLATE 16. David Hume.

PLATE 17. Thomas Muir.

PLATE 18. Henry, 1st Viscount Melville.

2. What happened to imports and re-exports of tobacco (*a*) between 1755 and 1775 (*b*) between 1775 and 1777?
3. (*a*) What event in America caused the result in 2(*b*)?
   (*b*) Which two European countries were Glasgow's best customers for tobacco?
   (*c*) Why were tobacco traders known as *the Tobacco Lords*?

The Clyde

Ships could not sail up the river as far as Glasgow until John Golborne succeeded in deepening it, principally by narrowing its channel, in the 1770's and Glasgow became its own port:

A defect, not easily remedied, is the shallowness of the river, which will not float vessels of any burden within ten or twelve miles of the city, so that the merchants are obliged to load and unload their cargoes at Greenock and Port Glasgow.

TOBIAS SMOLLETT, *Humphrey Clinker* [Fiction], 1771

From a sounding of the River Clyde, from the lower end of Dumbuckford to the Broomielaw, it now appears that the river is more than seven feet water at an ordinary neap tide and that Mr. Golborne, engineer, has fully implemented his contract with the city of Glasgow.

Scots Magazine, p. 693, 1775

Town and Trade

Despite the loss of the tobacco trade, Glasgow grew in population and area, its merchants busily engaged in international trade and manufacturers and workers in and around the city increasing production, especially in the cotton industry:

The old town lies on the declivity of a hill, chiefly beneath the cathedral. The commencement of the new town is to be dated soon after the union of the two kingdoms. It has kept gradually descending from the old one to the river, the source of its being, its commerce and its prosperity. Having at length reached the Clyde, it has continued spreading eastward along its banks to a breadth of three quarters of a mile on the right; and now taking in the village of Anderston, extends over two miles in length. Every part of this large space is not equally covered with houses at present; but probably will be in a few years. The rate of building perhaps out-runs the increase of inhabitants, now computed at sixty thousand.

I. LETTICE, *Tour*, in *Scots Magazine*, p. 391, 1794

The Coffee Room of the Tontine is 72 feet in length, and of a proportional breadth, and is universally allowed to be the most elegant in Britain, and possibly in Europe. Its main entry is from the Town House or Exchange.

Subscribers (900–1,000 of them in 1804) of £1 5s per annum, are entitled to the use of the room, newspapers and magazines, of which no Coffee Room in Britain can boast a greater variety. For here are not only the whole Scotch papers, but also the greater part of those published in London, as well as some from Ireland, France, etc. besides reviews, magazines and other periodical publications. At the daily arrival of the mail, a more stirring, lively and anxious scene can hardly be imagined.

Here you are not offended as in London, and several other towns, upon entering places of this description, with clouds of smoke and fumes of tobacco, or with that brutal noise, proceeding from the too free use of liquor; neither of which is allowed to be used in the room.

J. DENHOLM, History of Glasgow, pp. 189–91, 1804

The principal articles of exportation from Glasgow, and the ports farther down the river, to America and the West Indies, are British manufactures, also coal, fish, etc. To the Continent of Europe, and the ports in the Baltic, besides British manufactures, raw and refined sugar, coffee, cotton and rum.

Glasgow imports from the West Indies and America, the principal articles of growth and manufacture there, such as coffee, cotton, sugars, rum, mahogany, and flour; from Spain and Portugal, wines; from the Baltic, wood, iron, flax, hemp, pitch, tar, Russian linens and wheat.

Amongst all these articles of import, however, the principal are sugar, rum, coffee, cotton; the sugar and rum, besides serving the consumpt of the country, is exported again in great quantities, and often even to England for the use of the navy, the merchants here sometimes entering into the government contracts for that purpose. The cotton not only supplies the extensive cotton manufactures in Scotland, but is sent to Manchester, Liverpool and other towns in England, as well as to the Continent.

J. DENHOLM, History of Glasgow, pp. 410–11, 1804

1. (*a*) Who was the engineer who deepened the Clyde?
   (*b*) What value did this have for Glasgow?
2. (*a*) Why did Lettice regard the Clyde as 'the source of Glasgow's being'?
   (*b*) What was happening to the size of the city of Glasgow in the 1790's?
3. (*a*) Find out the meaning of: Tontine; Town House.
   (*b*) What sort of men would use the Tontine?

4. (*a*) Make lists of Glasgow's principal imports and exports.
   (*b*) Which commodity formerly the source of Glasgow's wealth has obviously lost its importance?

To guide your writing.
1. Why could Glasgow claim to be the commercial capital of Scotland?
2. Explain the factors which caused Glasgow to expand suddenly and swiftly between 1760 and 1820. (See also the sections on cotton and canals for further information.)
3. If you live in Glasgow, study a street map for names which suggest (*a*) early industries and (*b*) places abroad with which Glasgow merchants traded.

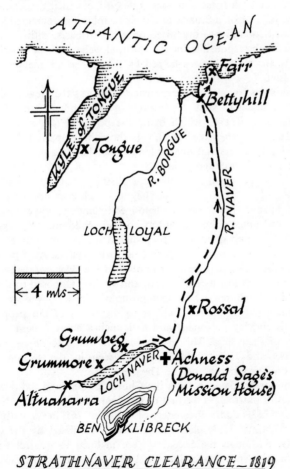

STRATHNAVER CLEARANCE—1819

8 · THE CHURCH

The Appointment of Ministers

After the Union of 1707 nearly all the people of Scotland belonged to the Presbyterian Church, the established Church of Scotland. True, the Episcopalian Church still had some support, especially in Aberdeenshire and among the nobility elsewhere, while parts of the Highlands remained Catholic, but both these churches suffered from their association with the cause of the exiled Stuarts and their membership remained low. The Church of Scotland was organised on a parish basis, with the minister of each church responsible for the spiritual welfare of the people in his parish. In his work, he was helped by the elders, the members of the Kirk Session.

But who was to appoint the minister? This was the great controversy which threatened to split the Church of Scotland. It arose from the Patronage Act of 1712 which made the powerful landowner in each parish the *lay patron* of the parish, with the right to appoint the minister. Previously, the elders and smaller landowners had had the right to 'call' a minister for their congregation.

It is not surprising that by the year 1760 most of the ministers were supporters of lay patronage since they had each been appointed by the local lay patron. They sometimes belonged to landed families themselves, or had lived among them as tutors to their children. Although many were scholarly and good men, they shared the worldly interests of the nobility and were anxious not to offend their masters. As supporters of the existing order, they became known as the *Moderates*, and under them the Church lost its enthusiasm and vitality. Opposed to them, but still within the Church, was a small group of ministers, who were generally poorer and stricter, but closer to the needs of the people, who wanted to end lay patronage and to launch a church crusade against the evils of their time. This group was known as the *Evangelicals* or *High-flyers* and their outlook can be seen in the section in this chapter on The Church and the Theatre.

Two minor breakaways from the Church of Scotland did occur over the matter of patronage: the first or Original Secession, led by Ebenezer Erskine in 1733, and the Presbytery of Relief in 1761, in sympathy with a minister, Thomas Gillespie, who had been dismissed by the General Assembly. Although the Seceders were inclined to quarrel with one another and to split further into rival groups, their sincerity won them much popular support and their numbers grew. The Moderates continued in power in the Church of Scotland for another seventy years but lay patronage proved to be a major cause of the Disruption in 1843 when over 450 ministers broke away and formed the Free Church of Scotland:

The Patronage Act

In 1712, Tory statesmen were in office. Tory squires formed five-sixths of this House. It was determined to restore to the old patrons the rights which had been taken away in 1690. The bill passed this House before the people of Scotland knew that it had been brought in. Then came a petition from a committee of the General Assembly. But party feeling ran high: public faith was disregarded: patronage was restored. To that breach of the Treaty of Union are to be directly ascribed all the divisions that have since rent the Church of Scotland.

Macaulay, Speech in House of Commons, July, 1845, quoted by JAMES RANKIN in *Handbook of the Church of Scotland*, pp. 230–1, 1888

Ministers and Patronage

Ministers realised that they had to cultivate the support of patrons but sometimes being 'the laird's man' created difficulties for a minister in his new parish:

I stayed over Sunday and preached to his Grace, the Duke of Argyll, who always attended the Church at Inveraray. The ladies told me that I had pleased his Grace, which gratified me not a little, as without him no preferment could be obtained in Scotland.

ALEXANDER CARLYLE, *Autobiography*, p. 400

In June 1770, I married. From the low income from the stipend of my church at Minto, there appeared a necessity for the immediate exertions of my friends to secure a more remunerative appointment for me. Sir Gilbert Elliot of Minto secured me the succession to Jedburgh. This was an instance of singular good fortune. The situation was healthy and pleasant, the stipend the highest in the presbytery, yet the duties were not more burdensome than in most country parishes.

THOMAS SOMERVILLE, *My Own Life and Times*, pp. 167–8

THE PLACING OF MR. BALWHIDDER: My placing was a great affair: for I was put in by the patron and the people knew nothing whatsoever of me and they did all that lay in the compass of their power to keep me out, insomuch that there was obliged to be a guard of soldiers to protect the presbytery. It was a thing that made my heart grieve when I heard the drum beating and the fife playing as we were going to the kirk. The people were really mad and vicious, and flung dirt at us as we passed and held out the finger of scorn at me.

When we got to the kirk door, it was found to be nailed up, and we were, therefore, obligated to go in by the window, and the crowd followed us in a most unreverent manner, making the Lord's house like an inn on a fair day, with their grievous yellyhooing. During the induction, Thomas Thorl, the weaver, got up and protested,

'Verily, verily, I say unto you, he that entereth not by the door into the sheepfold, but climbeth up some other way, the same is a thief and a robber.'

Although my people received me in this unruly manner, I resolved to cultivate civility among them and the very next morning I began a round of visitations. I found the doors in some places barred against me and I walked about from door to door like a dejected beggar, till I got a civil reception from no less a person than Thomas Thorl that had been so bitter against me in the kirk the foregoing day. He had seen me going about from house to house and in what manner I was rejected. He said to me in a kind manner, 'Come in, Sir, and ease yoursel. This early visitation is a symptom of grace that I couldna' have expectit frae a bird out of the nest of patronage.' We had some solid conversation together and quoth he, 'I was mindit never to set my foot within the kirk door while you were there; but no to condemn without a trial, I'll be there next Lord's day and egg my neighbours to be likewise, so ye'll no have to preach just to the bare walls and the laird's family.'

JOHN GALT, *Annals of the Parish*, p. 5 [Fiction]

1. Why do you think the House of Commons was debating patronage in 1845?
2. Find the meaning of: General Assembly; Presbytery; preferment; stipend; 'a bird out of the nest of patronage'.
3. Why was Mr. Balwhidder made so unwelcome in his new parish?
4. What action by the minister helped to make the people accept him?

The case for the Moderates

Alexander Carlyle, one of the leading Moderate ministers, believed that they did a great deal to keep the people loyal:

No country has ever been more tranquil, except the trifling insurrections of 1715 and '45, than Scotland has been since the Revolution of 1688 – a period of 117 years; while at the same time the country has been prosperous, with an increase of agriculture, trade, and manufactures to a degree unexampled in any age or country. How far the steady loyalty to the Crown, and attachment to the constitution, together with the unwearied diligence of the clergy in teaching a rational religion, may have contributed to this prosperity, cannot be exactly ascertained; but surely enough appears to entitle them to the high respect of the State, and to justice from the country, in a decent support to the ministers and to their families.

ALEXANDER CARLYLE, *Autobiography*, pp. 527–8

Thomas Somerville, the minister of Jedburgh, supported this view, pointing to his work after the outbreak of the French Revolutionary War (1793):

I felt it to be my duty to visit the families of my parishioners and by simple arguments to guard them against delusions about the French Revolution, which would destroy their present and future happiness.

THOMAS SOMERVILLE, *My Own Life and Times*, p. 264

The Laird of Cawdor in the 1770's feared the people's claim to call their own minister as much as he hated the enthusiastic spirit of the Evangelicals who supported it:

I think the popular calls are very absurd things, and the gentlemen by giving in to them increase the pride and insolence of the clergy and encourage a turbulent disposition among the common people. True national religion is the best thing in the world, but superstition and enthusiasm are two of the worst and most mischievous.

G. BAIN, *History of Nairnshire*, p. 291

The case against the Moderates

Robert Mitchell, in his *Memories of Ayrshire*, reckoned that most truly religious people had left the Church of Scotland and become Seceders:

The national church was in a declining and unsatisfactory state about 1780. Her doctrine was greatly corrupted, her discipline much relaxed, and patronage, supported when necessary by military affray, was oppressively exercised. Many excellent persons doubtless were still found in the church, as well as a number of godly and evangelical ministers, but they were few compared with the amount of others, e.g. those who had taken refuge in the churches of the Secession, of the Relief, etc.

Memories of Ayrshire, p. 301

1. Find the meaning of: insurrection; constitution; rational; popular.
2. State in your own words why the Laird of Cawdor was opposed to 'popular calls'.

To guide your writing.

1. Write a speech (*a*) to be delivered by a Moderate minister in favour of lay patronage; and another (*b*) by an Evangelical minister opposing it.
2. Once you have read all the sections on the Church, discuss the effects of the supremacy of the Moderates on the Church and the people.

The Church and the Lives of the People

Responsibility for the Poor

As we have seen (in Standards of Living) the second half of the eighteenth century was a time when prices rose. Workers' wages also increased, but for those who had no work, or were ill or old, life became very difficult. Their plight proved to be beyond the small resources of the parish church:

The number of poor families is about thirty. The burden of maintaining the poor falls almost entirely on tenants, tradesmen, servants and charitable persons attending the church, while other people, however rich, particularly non-resident heritors, whatever their income may be, contribute little or nothing. Hence there is, in general, ample ground for the common observation, 'that it is the poor in Scotland who maintain the poor'.

> *O.S.A.*, vol. 2, p. 112, Mauchlin, Ayrshire

The number on the poor's list is seventy and a very small fund allotted for their relief is divided quarterly among them. In this parish there is hardly any fund but the collections made in the church: and as very few indeed of the heritors reside in the parish, this seldom exceeds £10 per annum, from which there is a deduction of £2 10s 0d to the Session-clerk, and a very considerable one for bad half-pence collected: so that the share of each poor person must be very small.

The poor's funds, in most parishes in the north of Scotland, are very inadequate, and few more so than this one. It is much to be wished that some plan could be devised for the increase of funds for the relief of the poor, without subjecting the kingdom to the heavy burden of a general tax.

> *O.S.A.*, vol. 2, pp. 561-2, Rosskeen, Ross-shire

The poor beg from house to house. The begging poor have a share of everything the tenants can afford: meal, wool, milk, etc. They go about twice or thrice a year, lay by a little, then apply to spinning or some little industry, to procure for themselves some of the necessaries of life. It would be thought unkind to refuse an alms, or a night's quarters to a poor person – There are a great many beggars from other places.

O.S.A., vol. 2, pp. 454–5, Fortingal, Perthshire

The societies and corporations (bonnet-makers, skinners, tailors, shoemakers, and weavers) are of great service in maintaining their distressed members, and keeping them from being a burden on the public. They distribute annually among their poor brethren £180.

The number of poor who are on the pension list and receive weekly alms from the Kirk Session is eighty. They can only receive from 6d to 1s each, which, although it may assist them a little, is by no means able to support them in their own houses. Begging, therefore, is allowed and is a great burden on the inhabitants. The poor will never be suitably provided for until the proprietors of land agree to assess themselves in a sum that may be adequate to this purpose.

O.S.A., vol. 2, pp. 91–2, Kilmarnock

The regular provision for the poor of this parish is very liberal, amounting to £348. The family of the Duke of Hamilton give very handsome donations.

About the year 1750, the inhabitants, in order to put a stop to begging, and to give more regular relief to the modest poor, assessed themselves in the payment of annual poor's rates, the amount of which was then about £100. With this and the other funds, all the poor (then upwards of fifty) were decently supported and begging was strictly prohibited for a time. Claimants for public charity, however, becoming more numerous, the list was afterwards increased to 115 and the annual rates to £230.

There are also ten charitable institutions, formed by people of different occupations and professions for the relief of any of their numbers who may fall into distress. The most important of these are the weavers, who give to each of their members, while on a bed of sickness, 3s weekly, and when in a state of convalescence but unable to work 2s. It is needless to dwell here on the many benefits which would accrue both to the public and to individuals if such societies were more universal.

The number of beggars, belonging to this parish, is trifling compared to the crowds of vagrants of every description who swarm from the populous towns around, and spread over the country, begging, cheating, swindling or stealing, as best suits their purpose.

O.S.A., vol. 2, p. 204, Hamilton

1. Make sure you know what is meant by: non-resident heritors; Session-clerk; alms; vagrants.
2. (a) In the first two places, from whom did the money for the poor come?

    (b) Who collected the money and gave it to the poor? (See the second and fourth extracts.)

3. (a) Why did poor people have to beg?

    (b) How did the people of Hamilton try to stop begging in 1750?

    (c) Why do you think Fortingal had more than its fair share of beggars?

4. (a) What other help was available to some of the poor in towns like Kilmarnock and Hamilton compared with poor people in rural parishes?

    (b) What solutions to the problem of the poor were suggested by the ministers of (i) Kilmarnock and (ii) Hamilton?

The Church and People's Behaviour

The Church had authority over a much wider range of activities in the eighteenth century than it does today. Before the creation of the Welfare State, it did what it could to help the poor; before State education was introduced, ministers supervised and inspected parish schools; before there was a police force, the Church was the supervisor of public conduct and the judge of sin.

The elders took their duties seriously, as Andrew Melville commanded in the *Second Book of Discipline* (1578), 'to watch diligently upon the flock to their charge, baith publickly and privately, that na corruption of religion or manners enter therein'. They sought out evil with zeal and reported on everyone who strayed from the path of virtue. They came to think that goodness lay in obeying the Church's strict rules rather than positively doing good to their fellow men:

RESPECTING THE SABBATH DAY: Taking into consideration that the Lord's Day is profaned by people standing in the streets, wandering in the fields and gardens, as also by idly gazing out at windows, and children and apprentices playing in the streets, warn parents and order each Session to take its turn in watching the streets on the Sabbath, as has been the custom in this city, and to visit each suspected house in each parish.
Kirk Session of Edinburgh, 1709. *The King's Pious Proclamation* (1727), p. 79 quoted by H. G. GRAHAM, *Social Life of Scotland in the 18th Century*. p. 317

On looking from the windows we saw the grave Presbyterians with downcast looks, like conscience-stricken sinners, slowly crawling towards their place of gathering. We were admonished that it was not lawful to go forth to walk purposely on the Sabbath, a day of rest and worship.

After this serious warning, we sometimes found ourselves without [i.e. outside] the house on a Sunday and walked about a little, as by mere accident in Princes Street, when Shelley laughed aloud, with a fiendish laugh, at some remark of mine.

'You must not laugh openly, in that fashion, young man,' an ill-looking fellow said to him. 'If you do, you will most certainly be convened.'

'What is that?' asked Shelley, rather displeased.

'Why, if you laugh aloud in the public streets and ways on the Christian Sabbath, you will be cast into prison, and eventually be banished from Scotland.'

T. J. HOGG, *Life of Shelley*, p. 260, 1906

Rose at 7 in the morning, prayed then joined in family worship, and then read the 2nd chapter of Job. I went to God in prayer . . . Went to North West Church and heard Mr. M'Laurin lecture and preach. At home wrote down some head(ing)s of the sermon. Went to Church in the afternoon; heard sermon on same text as forenoon; returned and thought over the sermon till 5 o'clock; joined in family worship: supped and retired; thought over the sermon again and wrote down the heads of it (then prayer, family worship and Bible reading). Then I committed my soul and all my concerns to God and went to bed at 12 o'clock.

Diary of GEORGE BROWN, merchant, 1745–53

1. Who watched the streets of Edinburgh on the Sabbath?
2. State two offences which Shelley had committed.
3. What kind of activities filled George Brown's Sunday?

PUBLIC CONDUCT: The Kirk Session would impose fines on wrong-doers in minor cases and subject them to public disgrace for serious offences, by making them appear before the congregation, Sunday after Sunday, dressed in sack-cloth on the pillory or the 'stool of repentance':

In 1723 A. G. and J. R. were found guilty of unseemly behaviour in laughing and throwing stones in time of worship, and of cutting and giving one another apples in church: to appear four times before the Session meetings and pay 40s Scots.

GORDON, *Chronicles of Keith*, p. 100

In Banff about 1754, four offenders were usually standing together each Sunday on pillory.

Annals of Banff, vol. II, p. 77

Other common offences were swearing and brawling but seldom is drunkenness reported. Elders, however, combed the streets at night and sent people home, making sure that they kept 'elders' hours'.

Most of these cases of strict discipline by the Church occurred before

1760. Under the influence of Moderate ministers the Church loosened its grip on the people, although here and there some people, including Robert Burns, suffered the shame of the 'stool of repentance'. The easing of discipline is reported in the *Annals of the Parish* [Fiction]:

In conformity with the altered fashions of the age, in 1804 the Session came to an understanding with me that we should not continue the common church punishments. We laid it down as a rule to ourselves that in the case of transgressions on the part of the inhabitants of the new district of Cayenneville, who were irreligious, we should subject them rigorously to a fine; but for the farming lads, we would put it in their option to pay the fine or stand in the Kirk.

1. What is meant by 'elders' hours'; 'stool of repentance'?
2. In what way was discipline eased, according to the extract from *Annals of the Parish*?

THE CHURCH AND DRINK: Drunkenness came to the Lowlands with cheap whisky late in the eighteenth century and ministers feared the effects on the people:

It is not twenty-five years ago when almost nothing but ale brewed in the town was drunk by the tradespeople. The general use of whisky is arrived at an alarming rate among the lower ranks of people.

O.S.A., vol. 13, p. 438, Dumfermline

It is utterly impossible that spirits can remain at their present price (about three shillings the gallon in retail) without becoming the beverage of the common people.

O.S.A., vol. 10, p. 71, Kirkliston

There are thirty-two shops for the sale of spirits in this parish, which is just thirty too many. It is just so many persons scattered over the parish with their families and relations, whose living depends on the success with which they can prevail on their neighbours to drink. One man is paid for teaching sobriety, but thirty-two have an interest in defeating his efforts, and human nature is on their side.

N.S.A., vol. 1, p. 27, Liberton

1. Why was the problem of drink so much more serious in this period than earlier in the eighteenth century?
2. (a) Who was the 'one man paid for teaching sobriety'?
   (b) Why did he think he was fighting a losing battle?

THE CHURCH AND THE THEATRE: After the Reformation, the Presby-

terian Church in Scotland forbade the acting of religious plays and by
the eighteenth century many ministers and elders saw the theatre as the
agency of the Devil and all his works, corrupting men's minds and in-
sulting God's name. The scandal of a play having been written by a
Church of Scotland minister (*Douglas* by John Home) and watched and
enjoyed by large audiences, including ministers, brought the question of
the Church's attitude to the theatre to a head:

The play had unbounded success for a great many nights in Edinburgh
in 1756. The town in general was thrilled that a Scotsman had written a
tragedy of the first rate and that its merit was first submitted to their
judgement.

The High-flying set were unanimous against it, as they thought it a
sin for a clergyman to write any play.

ALEXANDER CARLYLE, *Autobiography*, p. 327

Carlyle, the minister of Inveresk and a friend of John Home the
author, has supported and attended the play and was summoned before
the Presbytery:

Mr. Alexander Carlyle did without necessity keep company, familiarly
converse and eat and drink with West Digges (one of the actors on the
unlicensed stage or theatre in Edinburgh called the Concert Hall), or
converse with Miss Sarah Ward, an actress, or with others who are in
the course of acting plays and who by their profession and in the eyes
of the law are of bad fame; and he did not only appear publicly in the
said unlicensed theatre, but took possession of a box, and did there
witness the acting of the tragedy called *Douglas*, when acted for hire or
reward, in which the name of God was profaned or taken in vain by
mock prayers and tremendous oaths, such as 'by the blood of the Cross'.

Presbytery of Dalkeith, quoted by ALEXANDER
CARLYLE, *Autobiography*, pp. 335–6,

John Home resigned from his church and Alexander Carlyle had to
apologise to the Presbytery. The General Assembly then offered these
words of advice to Presbyteries, 'that they take care that none of the
ministers of this Church do upon any occasion attend the theatre.'

The Moderates had been disciplined but theirs was the final victory:

In the year 1784, when the great actress Mrs. Siddons first appeared
in Edinburgh, during the sitting of the General Assembly, that court was
obliged to fix all its important business for the alternate days when she
did not act, as all the younger members, clergy as well as laity, took
their stations in the theatre on those days by three in the afternoon.

ALEXANDER CARLYLE, *Autobiography*, p. 339

In some places, however, ministers like John Galt's Mr. Balwhidder might want to attend plays but thought it better to stay away:

In August 1795, a gang of play actors came and hired Thomas Thacklan's barn. Their first performance was *Douglas Tragedy* and *The Gentle Shepherd.* The whole pack was in a state of perfect beggary and yet for all that, they not only in their parts, as I was told, laughed most heartily, but made others do the same; for I was constrained to let my daughter go to see them, with some of her acquaintances; and she gave me such an account of what they did, that I thought that I would have liked to have gotten a keek at them myself. At the same time I must own this was a sinful curiosity and I stifled it to the best of my ability.

JOHN GALT, *Annals of the Parish*, pp. 212-13 [Fiction]

1. What is the meaning of: High-flying set; profaned; laity?
2. What were the offences for which Alexander Carlyle was summoned before the Presbytery?
3. How did the younger members of the General Assembly feel about (*a*) the theatre and (*b*) the work of the General Assembly?

To guide your writing.
1. Explain why some people were so very poor in the 1790's.
2. As if you were a minister then, explain why the churches have become unable to cope with the problem of poverty and consider how you would try to care for the poor of your parish.
3. Consult the *Old Statistical Account* and report on the provision made for the poor in your parish in the 1790's.
4. What benefits are provided by the State today to help to banish poverty?
5. Give an account of the Church's aims, agents and methods in its task of regulating public behaviour in the eighteenth century.
6. Write a conversation between two elders in 1800 on whether it is wise to reduce the Church's authority and give people more freedom.
7. Try to justify the High-fliers' condemnation of the theatre.
8. Try to find out more about the play, *Douglas*, and the actress, Mrs. Siddons.
9. Do you think the Church's attitude has hampered Scotland's contribution to the acting and writing of plays?

Religion as Seen by Poets

The Sabbath

Robert Fergusson notices that people changed more than their clothes on that day:

On Sunday here, an alter'd scene
O' men and manners meets our ein:
Ane wad *maist trow* some people chose   [almost believe
To change their faces wi' their clo'es
And fain wad *gar* ilk neighbour think   [make
They thirst for goodness, as for drink.

ROBERT FERGUSSON, Auld Reekie

My Congregation

Our girls are dressed in cloak and gown
And think themselves quite bonny
Each comes on Sunday to the Kirk
In hopes to see her Johnny

A drover when the sermon's done
Will ask the price of cows
But the good honest Christian
Will stick to Gospel news.

REV. LACHLAN MACKENZIE, Minister of Lochcarron,
O.S.A., vol. 13, p. 560

The Holy Fair

This was a great outdoor service when Communion was given to
hundreds of people. It began with a Wednesday or Thursday fast, followed by preparatory services on Saturday, and on Sunday, minister
after minister preached to the people in the Churchyard from morning
till late at night. While this was going on, people went in relays into the
church to take Communion. Robert Burns describes the thoughts of
such a congregation in 'The Holy Fair'.

Here some are thinking on their sins,
And some upon their claes;
Ane curses feet, that *fyl'd* his shins,   [soiled
Anither sits an' prays:
On this hand sits a chosen *swatch*   [sample
Wi' screw'd-up, grace-proud faces
On that, a set o' chaps, at watch
Thrang winkin' on the lasses.   [busy

The Self-righteous Elder

Burns mocks 'Holy Willie', an elder who saw himself as a model
Christian, and prayed that his enemies would suffer and he prosper:

I bless and praise Thy matchless might
When thousands Thou has left in night
That I am here before Thy sight
    For gifts an' grace
A burning and a shining light
    To a' this place.

Yet I am here, a chosen sample,
To show Thy grace is great and ample;
I'm here a pillar o' Thy temple,
    Strong as a rock,
A guide, a buckler and example
    To a' Thy flock!

But, Lord, remember me and mine
Wi' mercies temporal and divine,
That I for grace and gear may shine,
    Excelled by nane!
And a' the glory shall be Thine!
    Amen, Amen!

From ROBERT BURNS, *Holy Willie's Prayer*

1. What is suggested about people and religion in the first three passages?

To guide your writing.

1. Read all of 'Holy Willie's Prayer' and other poems Burns wrote on religion such as 'Address to the Unco Guid' and see whether it was the Church or only certain people in it that he attacked.
2. How do you think the Church would be affected by the popularity of Burns's poems?

300 POUNDS REWARD.

WHEREAS, certain Wicked, Evil-disposed, and Traitorous Persons, during the night of the 1st, or on the morning of the 2d of April instant, did FELONIOUSLY, TRAITOROUSLY, and DARINGLY, in furtherance of a CONSPIRACY to compass or imagine the Death of Our Lord the King, or to LEVY WAR AGAINST OUR LORD THE KING, within his Realm, or to commit other Treasons, PUBLISH and AFFIX, on the walls and public places in many parts of the City and Suburbs of Glasgow, and other parts of the County of Lanark, a most WICKED, REVOLUTIONARY and TREASONABLE ADDRESS to the Inhabitants of Great Britain and Ireland, dated at Glasgow, April 1, 1820, and bearing to be issued "by order of the Committee of Organization for forming a Provisional Government," directly and openly PROCLAIMING REBELLION AGAINST OUR LORD the KING AND THE LAWS AND CONSTITUTION OF HIS REALM, inciting and stimulating the Subjects of our Lord the King to take up Arms for the overthrow of the Government and Constitution, as by Law established, and TO LEVY WAR AGAINST OUR LORD THE KING —and further endeavouring to seduce the Soldiers of our Lord the King to desert their duty and to join in a threatened Insurrection, and to intimidate and overawe all loyal and peaceable Subjects by threats of violence and devastation,—The LORD PROVOST and MAGISTRATES of the City of Glasgow, SHERIFF of the County of Lanark, and JUSTICES of the PEACE for the Lower Ward of Lanarkshire, hereby offer a

REWARD OF
THREE HUNDRED POUNDS

to any Person or Persons who shall, within fourteen days from this date, DISCOVER and APPREHEND, or cause to be DISCOVERED and APPREHENDED, those guilty of THIS OVERT ACT OF HIGH TREASON, by printing, publishing, and issuing the said Revolutionary and Treasonable Address, under the said Treasonable designation of the Committee of Organization for forming a Provisional Government.

Glasgow, 4th April, 1820.

---

as follows, viz.:—

At HAMILTON, on Saturda April, and within the New Hamilto Toll Bars at

ELVANFOOT,
ABINGDON,
DOUGLASMILN,
MILTON LESMAHA
CANDERDIKEHEAI
AVON BRIDGE,

in the County of Lanark; together with the respective Side Ba several Tolls.

The roup will begin at 12 o'clock dues and abstracts of the articles, the Toll Bars, and at the place of t Graham and Davidson, writers in G

Intending tacksmen must bring with them, or sufficient letters for that offers will not be received.

RENFREWSH

There will be let, by public roup, WITHIN the RENFREWSH at Paisley, on Thursday 1820, the TOLL DUTIES leviabl viz:—

Paisley East Bar,	Over Jo
Paisley West Bar,	Deafhill
Renfrew Bar,	Bridge
Blackhall,	Bridge
Causeyside,	Auchen
Hillington,	Lochwi
Clerksbridge,	Dunsm
Inchinnan,	Livingf
Barnsford,	Hardga
Houstoun,	

All the BARS in the COUNTY of l otherwise specif

Within the TOLL HOUSE at t of GLASGOW, on Friday the 21st TOLLS leviable at that BAR, and

Muirhouses,	Ouplay,
The Two Bars at Pollok-	Clarkst
shaws,	Carmur
At Darnley,	Kingsw
Ducathall,	And D
Shelford,	

And on Saturday the 22d day Within the COUNCIL CHAMB The TOLLS levi

Bishopton,	Crawfo
Port-Glasgow,	Brackle
Clune Brae,	Commo

The BARS on the High and Low The entry to the Bars at Brackles and on the High and Laigh Gouroc

---

PLATE 19. This advertisement appeared in the *Glasgow Courier* for April 4, 1820. It was inserted by Glasgow magistrates during 'the Radical War' of that year. (See p. 140.)

PLATE 20. Sir Walter Scott.

PLATE 21. Robert Burns.

PLATE 22. Lord Braxfield.

PLATE 23. Lord Cockburn.

9 · EDUCATION

Most burghs had schools, many of them with a long history. The Education Act, passed by the Scottish Parliament in 1696, provided for a school to be established in every parish in the country, as John Knox had intended over a hundred years earlier. In the bigger parishes in the Highlands, where one school in each parish was not enough, the Society for Propagating Christian Knowledge had been answering this need since 1709 by opening schools with financial help from the Government. Besides, there were a considerable number of private schools. Anyone could start a school: success or failure depended on local needs and what parents thought of the private teacher's ability, especially when compared with the parish schoolmaster.

Control over education was exercised locally, by the town council over the burgh school, and by the minister and the landowners over the parish school. There was no central direction or inspection by the Government. The law laid down that there should be schools, but town councils and landowners were to pay for them. This arrangement served local needs fairly well until later in the eighteenth century when population increased and many people moved from rural parishes to industrial towns because of the agricultural and industrial revolutions. Then, the existing town schools could no longer cope with the larger number of children living there, and many new schools were required:

Attendance, Fees, Hours, Holidays

Education was seldom free and not compulsory but most parents appreciated the value of education and tried to send their children to school, at least for a time:

Into a small schoolroom, crowded with some threescore young commoners of both sexes, is led forward by the fond parent to the foot of the village teacher's small, old table-desk, our bare-headed little self, rising five years old, eyeing 'the Maister'. About my ninth year it was considered necessary that I should commence with my father his craft of a shoemaker.

JOHN YOUNGER, Shoemaker, *Autobiography*, pp. 5–7

At the parish school of Cromarty there attended about a hundred and twenty boys, with a class of about thirty individuals more, much looked down on by the others, seeing that it consisted of only *lasses*.

HUGH MILLAR, *My Schools and Schoolmasters*, p. 41

In a few instances the sons of private gentlemen were bred at home by a tutor: but the far greater part went to the neighbouring school every morning. They were none the worse for being bred with the sons of their country neighbours. They learned to estimate their neighbours with justice and liberality, not to consider them as animals of an inferior species.

RAMSAY OF OCHTERTYRE: a laird educated at Dalkeith Grammar School, *Scotland and Scotsmen in the Eighteenth Century*, vol. 2, p. 57

FEES	Parish School	– English	1s 4d per quarter
		Writing	2s per quarter
		Arithmetic	2s per quarter
		Latin	2s 6d per quarter

O.S.A., vol. 10, p. 247 Cluny

	Grammar School	– Reading, Writing	7s 6d per quarter
		and Arithmetic	(or 3s 6d each)
		Latin	5s per quarter
		Latin and Greek	7s 6d per quarter

Jedburgh Grammar School, 1808

HOURS   Glasgow Grammar (now High) – 7–9, 10–12, 1–3 in summer
School   9–11, 12–2,   in winter
                                                       (1782)

HOLIDAYS Jedburgh Grammar School – 1 month at harvest
                                    Friday afternoon and all
                                    Saturday at the end of each
                                    month.

1. How do these school arrangements with regard to attendance, fees, hours and holidays compare with modern schools?

Subjects Taught

Different kinds of schools taught different subjects but most schoolmasters had been to University and had studied Latin and Greek, and even in parish schools Latin was taught. It was possible for the clever boy, the 'lad o' pairts', to proceed straight from the parish school to university, to become a teacher, or perhaps a minister:

IN A PARISH SCHOOL – LONGNEWTON, ROXBURGHSHIRE: What an exertion of judgment and memory takes place, between the time we can certainly distinguish the letter O, 'round like the moon', till we have learnedly mastered the 'Reading made easy'. Our lesson reading was the Scriptures, first through the New, then the Old Testament. We imitated our teacher in writing particularly slow, which though a good mode for beginners, kept up an awkward stiffness in the writing.

About my ninth year, I had to leave. My parents thought that time might improve their circumstances and that I should get to school to my arithmetic at a future period, which never arrived.

JOHN YOUNGER, Shoemaker, *Autobiography*, pp. 5–7

IN A HIGH SCHOOL – EDINBURGH: This school was, like Glasgow Grammar School [now High School], an outstanding example of the classical tradition, the teaching of Latin and Greek. Many of the older burgh schools concentrated on these subjects:

[The work was] confined to Latin alone. Oh, the bodily and mental weariness of sitting six hours a day, staring idly at a page, without motion and without thought.

After four years of this class, I passed on to that of the rector, Doctor Alexander Adam. Never was a man more fortunate in his choice of vocation. He was born to teach Latin, Greek and all virtue. I remained in the rector's class two years. [He left before he was 14].

COCKBURN, *Memorials of His Time*, p. 4

IN AN ACADEMY – PERTH: Perth Acacemy, founded in 1760, pioneered the study of new subjects, as opposed to the privileged position held by Latin, e.g. in the High School of Edinburgh. Probably Jedburgh, the example given next, was influenced by the success of Perth:

The Academy for mathematics, astronomy and the several parts of education which are proper to fit young men for business, is well attended by students, even from distant countries. It has a rector, an assistant, a French master and a drawing master.

O.S.A., vol. 18, p. 538, Perth

IN A SMALL GRAMMAR SCHOOL – JEDBURGH: The range of subjects offered here is exceptionally wide, partly because the school is advertising for more pupils and may be trying to sell its wares, and partly because the school had joined with another in the town in 1803. Probably some pupils were only taught the 'three R's':

Subjects: Latin, Greek, French, Roman Antiquities, Geography, Writing, Arithmetic, Book-keeping, Navigation, Measuring, Trigonometry, Algebra, and English Language.

Advertisement in *Kelso Mail*, 1808

1. How would you sum up the subjects taught in the parish school of Longnewton?
2. What was the main subject in the High School of Edinburgh and what do you think was the aim in teaching it?

3. What new subjects were offered in Perth Academy and why?
4. Assuming that the subjects at the beginning of the advertisement list were the most important, what conclusion would you draw about the curriculum in Grammar Schools?

Discipline

A boy caught speaking a word of Gaelic was pretty sure to be made to mount the back of some one of his sturdier schoolmates and then, moving in a circuit around the master, tawse in hand, get soundly thrashed. You may well guess what a terror was inspired by such a punishment in the case of little urchins wearing the kilt.

> Kenmore, Argyll, about 1815, from EVAN MCCOLL, *Clarsach nam Beann*, p. 5

If a boy really wished to learn, the parish schoolmaster certainly could teach him. But, the pupils who wished to do nothing – and they comprised fully two thirds of the younger ones – were not required to do much more than they wished.

> Cromarty School, from HUGH MILLER, *My Schools and Schoolmasters*, p. 43

The person to whose uncontrolled discipline I was now subject though a good man, was as bad a schoolmaster as it is possible to fancy. Out of the whole four years of my attendance there were probably not ten days in which I was not flogged, at least once.

> High School of Edinburgh, from LORD COCKBURN, *Memorials of His Time*, p. 3

Sir,   February 1812
I am under the necessity of writing you of the behaviour of my scholars, which is very troublesome. J. and G. Murray never learn their lessons, and another is very noisy.
Please inform the scholars to behave better. If the noise continues, I shall return you the key of the school.

> I am, etc,
> Doubzere.

Sir,   March 1812
It is with great pleasure that I inform you of the good effect my letter produced. I must praise the hard work of Mr. G. Murray. I hope that the others will soon give me the same satisfaction.

> I am, etc,
> Doubzere.

Two letters to the Rector of Jedburgh Grammar School from

Doubzere, a French prisoner of war there, who had been engaged to teach French to the pupils.

1. What do you think brought about the great change in G. Murray's attitude to work?
2. For what offence was a pupil punished in this way at Kenmore?

Payment of Teachers

The salaries of parish schoolmasters were fixed in 1696 and were not improved for over a century even although the cost of living rose steeply:

IN PARISH SCHOOLS: There shall be a school established and a schoolmaster appointed in every parish. The heritors shall provide a commodious house for a school and shall settle a salary on the schoolmaster which shall not be under one hundred Merks (£5 11s 1d) nor above two hundred Merks [£11 2s 2d] a year to be paid yearly at two terms, Whitsunday and Martinmas by equal portions.

1696 Education Act

The money was to be raised by a levy on the heritors, depending on the value of their land. Account books often give examples of this, e.g:

To Thomas Wilson, schoolmaster of Kirktoun, proportion of the Schoolmaster's salary for his lands in Kirktoun parish from Martinmas 1773 to Martinmas 1774 . . . 8s $0\frac{8}{12}$d.

The salary of the parish schoolmaster is £9 9s 0d. This, with school fees, etc. makes the office of schoolmaster worth about £25 a year. There is a schoolhouse but no house for the schoolmaster.

When these salaries were originally fixed [in 1696] in Scotland they bore a reasonable proportion to the value of money, and to the price of labour and provisions, but since that time, every article of dress, provisions and household furniture is risen to a degree almost incredible; and a shilling in real value, is worth little more than a penny was then.

O.S.A., vol. II, pp. 168–9, Kilwinning, Ayrshire

It is much to be regretted that schoolmasters who generally get a university education and are a most useful class of men to the community, should be so miserably provided for as scarcely to have the necessities of life.

O.S.A., vol. 10, p. 247, Cluny

The 1803 Education Act gave schoolmasters their first official increase in salaries since 1696, to a minimum of £16 13s 4d and a maximum of

£22 4s 5d. Houses of not more than two rooms including the kitchen were to be erected for schoolmasters. This Act, according to Lord Cockburn, created an outcry among M.P.'s and landlords who were unwilling to erect 'palaces for dominies'.

IN OTHER SCHOOLS: A school is established in the lower part of Ardchattan parish by the Society for Propagating Christian Knowledge, with a salary of £13 sterling; and the schoolmaster's wife has from the Society £3 for teaching young girls to spin and knit stockings, which is of great benefit to the parish.

O.S.A., vol. 6, p. 179, Ardchattan and Muckairn, Argyll

To Mr. Lorrain,
Schoolmaster, Jedburgh.
Sir,   January 1, 1812
   I hereby acknowledge the receipt of thirteen pounds sterling which with other items makes thirty-five pounds, being payment in full of my last year's salary, for which I return you my sincere thanks and am,
                          Sir,
                              Your obedient servant,
                                  James Anderson, Assistant Master.

William Lorrain, Schoolmaster, Jedburgh.	September, 1808
Income from Salary and school fees	£70
Profits from boarders	£20
	———
	£90
	———
Full duty	£9
Allowance by the Act	£3
	—
Duty payable	£6
	—

1. These figures are from Mr. Lorrain's assessment for Property Tax, as it was called. As you can see it is based on his income and we would call it Income Tax. From the full duty of £9 on £90 calculate the rate per £ in 1808.
2. What is meant by: a dominie; a schoolhouse?
3. What other source of income did burgh and parish schoolmasters have besides their salaries?
4. (a) What evidence is given to prove that salaries were too low in the 1790's?
   (b) When was the Act which made schoolmasters better off?
5. Which schoolmasters were better off than parish schoolmasters?

To guide your writing.

1. Attendance at school:
   (*a*) Did most children have the opportunity to go to school in
        Scotland at this time?
   (*b*) Did they have to go to school?
   (*c*) Why did some leave early?
   (*d*) Try to find out what provision was made for education in
        England at that time.
2. Try to find out (*a*) who the heritors were (*b*) more about the
   Society for Propagating Christian Knowledge.
3. (*a*) Using the knowledge you have gained from these readings,
        imagine you were a pupil in a parish school and give an
        account of your day.
   (*b*) Do the same for a grammar school or academy.
4. Taking (*a*) Longnewton as typical of a parish school
          (*b*) Edinburgh High School as an old grammar school
          (*c*) Perth Academy as a pioneer of teaching 'new subjects'
   and (*d*) Jedburgh as a small burgh school, describe the kinds of
   schools which were provided in Scotland about the year 1800.
   What other schools were there?
5. Try to find out all you can about schools in your own town or
   parish at this time. The *Old Statistical Account*, quoted here,
   contains information about schools in every parish in Scotland in
   the 1790's.

10 · GOVERNMENT

Scottish Representation in the British Parliament

The Act of Union of 1707 marked the end of the independent Scottish parliament in Edinburgh and the addition of Scottish members to the English parliament in London, Forty-five Scottish M.P.'s were to join the 513 English and Welsh members in the House of Commons, and sixteen Scottish lords, elected by their fellows, were to enter the House of Lords. With one-twelfth of the M.P.'s that England had, Scotland was under-represented on grounds of population, but the number of members she was allowed was based on the comparative wealth of the two countries and the share the Scots were expected to contribute in taxes. The number of Scottish M.P.'s remained unchanged until 1832.

As the number of Scottish M.P.'s was so small in relation to their English counterparts, it was impossible for them to achieve much for Scotland's benefit against solid opposition from English members. In practice, because the number of voters was so small in both county and burgh, it proved fairly easy for a strong personality like Henry Dundas, Lord Melville, when he was a member of the Government, to use his influence to secure the election of Scottish M.P.'s who would support the party in power:

Counties

In the reign of James the Sixth of Scotland and First of England, the right of voting was first restricted to freeholders possessing lands of forty shillings of what was called 'old extent', that is of lands which were so rated in the cess or county-books about the end of the thirteenth century.

By an Act of Charles II, 1681, it was enacted that the right of voting should be in persons [with] property or superiority of lands of forty shillings old extent, or 400 pounds Scots valued rent. By an ingenious device of the lawyers, when a person of great property wishes to multiply his votes, he surrenders his charter to the Crown; he appoints a number of confidential friends to whom the Crown parcels out his estates in lots of 400 pounds Scots valued rent; then he takes charters from these friends for the real property, thus leaving them apparently the immediate tenants of the Crown, and consequently all entitled to vote or to be elected. (These are called fictitious voters or parchment barons.)

The total number of real voters in the counties is 1,390. The total of false, nominal or fictitious voters, 1,201: and thirty-three counties return only thirty members, six having only the right of sending a member to every second Parliament.

Example:

Midlothian: Population		122,954
Number of voters – fictitious	10
	total	34

Patron – Duke of Buccleuch

When the county of Caithness returns a member, he is nominated by Sir John Sinclair. The County of Cromarty is under the influence of Henry Davidson, Esq., and the County of Kinross, of Thomas Graham, Esq. The late Lord Melville always boasted that he could return thirty-nine out of forty-five who represented the whole kingdom of Scotland!

T. H. B. OLDFIELD, *The Representative History of Great Britain and Ireland* vol. vi, pp. 123–30, 147, 296, 1816

1. Explain clearly what is meant by: freeholder; 'old extent'; cess, fictitious voters or parchment barons.
2. What was the value of land which gave the right to vote,
    (*a*) in the reign of James VI and I?
    (*b*) in 1681?
3. What kind of people were the real voters?
4. (*a*) How many real voters were there in Midlothian?
    (*b*) Who benefited from the creation of fictitious voters?
5. (*a*) How many M.P.'s represented the Scottish counties?
    (*b*) How many real voters were there altogether in the counties of Scotland?
    (*c*) What was the average number of real voters per M.P.?
    (*d*) How does the number of fictitious voters compare, roughly, with the number of real voters?

(See the section on The Dundas Influence for Lord Melville and the return of loyal Scottish members.)

Cities and Burghs

The royal burghs in Scotland had for a long time had the privilege of self-government in local affairs through their own town councils. As the first paragraph of the following passage suggests, the election of town councils was undemocratic since the old council chose the new one, with some of the old members serving on it. With the exception of Edinburgh which had its own Member of Parliament, the royal burghs were arranged in groups and delegates chosen by each town council in the group met to choose the M.P. Other burgesses had no voice in his election but local landowners could usually influence the choice. The size of the royal burgh was not important: for example, Dumbarton chose a delegate just as Glasgow did. If a burgh was a royal foundation it was represented, but some big towns like Paisley which did not have royal charters were not represented as burghs at all:

By an act passed in 1469, the town councils were invested with the power of electing their successors; and in 1474, it was ordained that four persons of the old should be annually chosen into the new town councils. By these laws, the burgesses had no longer any control over their magistrates; and the corporations became self-elected, totally separated in interest from their former constituents and fellow-citizens.

At the Union, Edinburgh, being the capital, alone retained the right of sending one member to Parliament. All the other towns were thrown into districts of fours and fives, each district being allowed to send one member. Every burgh (council) now elects a delegate; these delegates meet by rotation at each of the towns to elect the representative. The place where they meet is called the presiding burgh for that election and its delegate has the casting vote in case of an equality of voices.

Glasgow's number of inhabitants exceeds 77,000; its delegate is chosen by thirty-two members of the town council, who are all self-elected; and this delegate has only one voice of four in the choice of a member of Parliament with the delegates of three little towns (Renfrew, Rutherglen, and Dumbarton).

Of fifteen members for the cities and burghs, one for Edinburgh is chosen by thirty-three persons; the other fourteen by sixty-five delegates, who are elected by 1,220 persons (who are all town councillors).

The inhabitants of Scotland are above two million; their representatives are chosen by 3,844. Scotland sends forty-five members; a single county in England, namely Cornwall, sends forty-four.

Examples:

    i. Edinburgh City – Population   67,000
                     Number of Councillors 33
                     Number of Voters   33
             Patrons – Duke of Buccleuch and Mr. Dundas
                     of Arniston, nephew of Lord Melville.

    ii. Glasgow, Renfrew, Rutherglen, Dumbarton
          Glasgow – Population   77,385
                     Number of Councillors 33
                     Number of delegates   1
          Renfrew – Population   2,031
                     Number of Councillors 21
                     Number of delegates   1
       Rutherglen – Population   2,437
                     Number of Councillors 19
                     Number of delegates   1

Dumbarton – Population   2,549
Number of Councillors 15
Number of delegates   1
∴ Total number of delegates to choose
member of parliament = 4

Patrons – Sir John Maxwell and Archibald Campbell, Esq.

T. H. B. OLDFIELD, *The Representative History of Great Britain and Ireland*, vol. VI, pp. 130–3, 165, 190–3, 1816

1. Explain clearly what is meant by: burgess; magistrate; corporation; delegate; casting-vote?
2. What did all the burgh voters have in common?
3. Name two constituencies in which the Duke of Buccleuch had some influence? (See also Counties.)

To guide your writing.

1. (*a*) What do you think was wrong with the system of electing M.P.'s in the counties?
   (*b*) Can you think of any argument in favour of it?
2. (*a*) Imagine you were an educated citizen of Glasgow but not a town councillor in 1816 and write a letter to the Press, criticising (*i*) how the Town Council is chosen and (*ii*) how your City is represented in Parliament.
   (*b*) Imagine you were the Lord Provost of Glasgow in 1816 and write a reply to 2(*a*).
3. Work out the wording for a poster, expressing the *main* grievances of the people of Scotland about their representation in Parliament in 1816. Try to do it with as few words as possible to achieve the greatest possible impact.
4. Look up the terms of the 1832 Reform Act for Scotland and find out how many of the old abuses were swept away.
5. Try to find out all the details you can about how your own burgh or county was represented in Parliament before 1832.

The Dundas Influence

The previous section showed that the number of voters in Scottish elections was small, so small that the result of an election could be swayed or, in some cases, settled by the authority of a single local landowner. Political power in Scotland was in the hands of a very few men.

For nearly twenty years after 1783, power over them was exercised skilfully by Henry Dundas, a Midlothian lawyer and landowner. Becoming an ally of the Younger Pitt, the Prime Minister, Dundas was rewarded with several important posts in the Government. He became Treasurer of the Navy, President of the India Board and after 1791, Home Secretary. As the most important Scotsman in Parliament and in the Government, he could use his position to reward those who supported him. He could grant promotion to young men in the Navy, award posts in the East India Company and secure pensions for their relatives and friends. Equally he could use his influence to block the ambitions of political enemies. He studied each constituency with care and cultivated the friendship of influential landowners who found it to their benefit to support candidates favoured by him.

His control of Scotland has been described as the 'Dundas Despotism' and he himself has been called 'King Harry the Ninth'. Most Scottish M.P.'s proved to be loyal supporters of the Younger Pitt's Government at this time, thanks to Dundas's success as the political 'manager' of Scotland.

Dundas's explanation of support for him in Scotland

When one finds oneself in possession of an interest founded partly on private friendship, partly on family connections, partly on the gratitude of friends whom he has had it in his power to oblige, and partly, I flatter myself, on grounds of a still more public nature, he is not fond of allowing it to be frittered away.

> Letter of Henry Dundas to Robert Baird, April 1795, quoted by
> H. FURBER, *Henry Dundas, 1st Viscount Melville*, p. 251

Sir Walter Scott's opinion

No one can carry Scotland that has not the command of the Board of Control [for India], which is in a manner the key of the corn-chest; for your ladyship knows all our live articles of exportation are our black cattle and our children and though England furnishes a demand for our quadrupeds we are forced to send our bipeds as far as Bengal.

> Sir Walter Scott to Lady Abercorn, *Letters of
> Sir Walter Scott,* vol. 2, p. 276, ed. GRIERSON

1. What different grounds does Dundas give for the support he gained?
2. How does Sir Walter Scott explain it?

Pension List of Scotland 1792

One hundred and seventy-five pensions were granted in 1792 at a total cost of £24,842. The highest sum paid was £600 each to Baroness Forrester and the Earl of Dunmore and the lowest £20 to be shared between

two sisters, Ann and Elizabeth Forbes. Most of the grants were to women
or children, only about thirty being to men. They include:

Lady Wallace, sister of Duchess of Gordon	£150
Lady Ann Gordon	£150
Lady Katharine Gordon	£150
Dr. Hugh Blair, 1st Prof. of Rhetoric, Edinburgh Univ.	£200
Dr. Adam Fergusson, Prof. of Moral Philosophy	£200
Mrs. Katherine Barnet, spouse of the said Dr. Adam Fergusson and Isabella, Mary and Margaret, his daughters	£100
Dr. James Beattie, author of *Enquiry after Truth*	£200
Wade Toby Cawlfield	£150
Children of deceased Lord Napier	£300
Lady Dalzell	£200
Mrs. Helen Menzies	£60
Mrs. Colonel Cunningham	£100
William, Earl of Home	£300

Scots Magazine, Dec. 4, 1792

Dundas defended his record in awarding pensions in a letter of 15th
Dec. 1803:

From the time I first came to have a lead in the affairs of Scotland, as
far back as the last years of Lord North's administration, the grants of
pensions on the Scottish establishments have been confined to persons
of rank whose fortunes are inadequate to their situation, and to men of
literature.

Even after Dundas (now Lord Melville) lost office in 1806, he had still
enough influence to look after those who received pensions:

Lord Melville, who time nor circumstances never change, came and
sat an hour with me in Edinburgh, and was the first person who told
me the pensions were to be restored.

Letter of Duchess of Gordon, Dec. 1807, quoted by
C. MATHESON, *Life of Henry Dundas, 1st Viscount
Melville*, p. 383

The award of pensions was often criticised, as this violent attack in
the *Edinburgh Gazetteer*, Nov. 16, 1792, illustrates:

Are a class of prejudiced, privileged persons – Peers, Pensioners,
Placemen and Courtiers – to keep the power of dictating to those by
whose patient industry, every comfort, every luxury of life, originates.
We think not. We are convinced of the oppressions that the country

labours under. The national debt of *two hundred and forty millions* proclaim them. Annual taxes to the amount of *seventeen millions*, confirm them. Yet the Pension List has considerably increased. Is this plan for providing for virtuous families in distress to be considered as a retaining fee for future, or as a remuneration for past services? This engine of corruption has always been employed as the distresses of the country have increased.

1. What social classes did the people named as receivers of pensions belong to?
2. Does Dundas's statement about the grants of pensions appear to be true, judging from the kind of people named in the list?
3. Judging from the Duchess of Gordon's letter, how would those who received pensions feel about Henry Dundas?
4. On what grounds does the writer in the *Edinburgh Gazetteer* criticise the Pension List?

Appointments

The following three extracts from letters by Robert Anstruther show how he helped Dundas and how he was rewarded:

When Mr. Henry Erskine [a Whig] stood for the county of Fife, I at Mr. Dundas's particular request engaged my own vote and what votes I could bring for Mr. Wemyss. (1788.)

My son, Philip, having passed for Lieutenant in the Navy early in this year, I applied to Mr. Dundas to get him appointed to a ship, which he in the most obliging manner promised, saying he should take care of the young man's promotion, as if he were his own son. In a few months a large appointment of Lieutenants took place and he was one of the number. (1790.)

I wrote to Mr. Dundas asking to get the same young man made Master and Commander. (1793.)

Quoted by H. FURBER, *Henry Dundas 1st Viscount Melville*, pp. 245–6

'We do not like him much here: we are never sure which side he will vote on.' This comment, made in London about George Dempster when he was an M.P. suggests that he was a man of independent mind. It is not surprising, therefore that he had difficulty in obtaining a favour from Dundas:

I wrote to Mr. Dundas on the subject of a Bengal voyage for my

brother, but have not been favoured with an answer. It would cost him
only mentioning the matter to any one of the Directors of the Committee of Correspondence. I mean mentioning it as a thing he wished.
The truth is the whole profits of the trade are now confined to the Bengal
voyages. A man may sail till he be grey-headed between Europe and the
other parts of India making only bare bread, but a voyage or two to
Bengal is still a fortune.

G. DEMPSTER, Letters to Sir Adam Fergusson, p. 187

A candidate was persuaded to withdraw from an election altogether
by the promise of the right to make appointments in the East India
Company. The candidate was John Peter Grant of Rothiemurchus, the
father of Elizabeth Grant, who described the incident in *Memoirs of a
Highland Lady*, p. 62:

My father canvassed Inverness against the East India Director, Charles
Grant, who to secure his seat promised my father unlimited Indian
appointments if he would give in. This was the secret of my father's
Indian patronage, through which he provided ultimately for so many
poor cadets.

1. (*a*) What did Robert Anstruther do for Henry Dundas in 1788?
   (*b*) What did Anstruther ask Dundas to do for him later?
2. (*a*) What was the attraction of a Bengal voyage?
   (*b*) Why, probably, was Dempster's application unsuccessful?
3. Find out the meaning of: canvassing; patronage; cadets?

The Climax

It appeared to me that if I came to Scotland and exerted myself
thoroughly, I might be able to prevent the return *of any one member for
Scotland hostile to the Government.*

H. DUNDAS, May 1796, quoted by C. MATHESON
in Henry Dundas, First Viscount Melville, p. 227

He did not quite achieve this, but he was sure of the support of at
least thirty-six out of forty-five.

To guide your writing.
1. Explain how Henry Dundas made himself so powerful in Scotland, mentioning (*a*) the use of pensions, (*b*) appointments and
   (*c*) control of elections.
2. As an enthusiastic Parliamentary reformer criticise Dundas's
   position of power and his methods.
3. Do you think (*a*) Dundas deserved to be called 'King Harry the

Ninth'? (*b*) Dundas's control of Scotland amounted to despotism? Give reasons for your answers.

Town Councils

As has already been noted in the section on Scottish Representation in the British Parliament, town councils in Scotland had the right to name their successors. Thus control over a town's land and other sources of income was in the hands of a very small group, until the passing of the Burgh Reform Acts in 1833:

Lord Provosts of Glasgow 1796–1816

1796 – James McDougall, Esq.	1806 – James McKenzie, Esq.
1798 – Laurence Craigie, Esq.	1808 – James Black, Esq.
1800 – John Hamilton, Esq.	1810 – John Hamilton, Esq.
1802 – Laurence Craigie, Esq.	1812 – Kirkman Finlay, Esq., M.P.
1804 – John Hamilton, Esq.	1814 – Henry Monteith, Esq., M.P.

J. STRANG, *Glasgow and its Clubs*, p. 360

Town Council of Nairn 1776

Hugh Rose of Kilravock.
Major-General Simon Fraser of Lovat.
Colonel Hector Munro of Novar.
Lewis Rose of Coulmony.
Captain Hugh Rose of Brea.
Alexander Rose in Flemington.
Hugh Rose of Aitnoch.
Alexander Baillie of Dochfour.
Mr. Hugh Falconer, Merchant in Nairn.
Mr. David Falconer there.
Alexander Ore of Knockondie.
Captain John Fraser in Geddes.
James Fraser of Gortulig, W.S.
Henry Mackenzie, Attorney in the Court of Exchequer.
Dr. John Alves, Physician in Inverness.
William Ballentine at Balloan.
Robert, Glass, Shoemaker in Nairn.

G. BAIN, *History of Nairnshire*, pp. 325–6

Nae langer thrifty citizens and douce
Meet owre a pint, or in the council-house;
But *staumrel*, corky-headed, graceless Gentry   [half-witted
The *herryment* and ruin of the country;   [plundering
Men, three parts made by tailors and by barbers,

Wha waste your weel-*hained* gear on d——d   [saved
new Brigs and Harbours!

ROBERT BURNS, *The Brigs of Ayr*

1. How many in the list of Glasgow Lord Provosts held that office
   more than once?
2. (*a*) How many members were there on Nairn Town Council?
   (*b*) How many have the surname of Rose; Fraser; Falconer?
   (*c*) If 'of' immediately after a man's surname indicates that he
       was a landowner, how many of Nairn's councillors were
       landowners?
   (*d*) How many had military rank?
   (*e*) Knowing that W.S., i.e. Writer to the Signet, means that a
       man was a lawyer, how many of the councillors were lawyers?
   (*f*) How many of this council actually lived in Nairn?
3. (*a*) What kind of people had gained control of Ayr Town Council,
       according to Burns?
   (*b*) Why did he criticise them?

Edinburgh Town Council

Inevitably town councillors were either members of the Merchant
Company or one of the incorporated trades, and in neither case did the
citizens have any voice in selecting them:

The council met in a low blackguard-looking room, very dark, and
very dirty, with some dens off it for clerks.

Within this Pandemonium sat the town council, omnipotent, corrupt,
impenetrable. Nothing was beyond its grasp, no variety of opinion
disturbed its unanimity, for the pleasure of Dundas was the sole rule for
every one of them. But the year 1799 disclosed the incredible fact that
the town council contained a member who had an opinion of his own.
A councillor, named Smith, electrified the city by a pamphlet showing
that the burgh was bankrupt. Time has put it beyond all doubt that he
was right; but his rebellion drove Smith out of his place.

The town council's two great organs were John Gray and James
Laing. Gray was city clerk; a judicious man with a belly, white hair, and
decorous black clothes; famous for drinking punch, holding his tongue
and doing jobs quietly; a respectable and useful officer, with such wisdom
and such intimate acquaintance with affairs that he was oftener the
master than the slave.

If Gray was the head of the town council, Laing was its hand. He was
one of the clerks and though not an officer in the old Town Guard,
could, as representing the magistrates, employ it as he chose. It is incredible how much power this man had and how much he was feared.

He had more sense than to meddle with the rich but over the people he tyrannised to his heart's content.

LORD COCKBURN, *Memorials of His Time*, pp. 70–73

1. Find the meaning of: pandemonium; omnipotent; corrupt; unanimity; bankrupt; decorous.
2. (*a*) Who was Dundas? (See Scottish Representation in the British Parliament.)
   (*b*) Why did the councillors nearly always think alike?
   (*c*) Who was the real master of the Town Council?

The Benefits of being a Town Councillor

When any public work was to be undertaken, a preference was given to councillors as a matter of course. Therefore the deacon of the masons (who was a town councillor of Edinburgh) claimed as a right to be employed as builder to the Corporation and to charge his own prices without check.

ROBERTSON and WOOD, *Castle and Town*, p. 188, 1928

Several leases came to an end in the year of eighty-eight, and among others, the Niggerbrae park, which might have been re-let with a rise and advantage. But what did the dean of guild do? He gave a hint to my lord's factor to make an offer for the park on a two nineteen years' lease, at the rent then going – which was done in my lord's name, his lordship being then provost. The Niggerbrae was accordingly let to him, at the same rent which the town received for it in 1769.

Nothing could be more manifest than that there was some jookerie-cookerie in this affair; but how the dean of guild's benefit was to ensue, no one could tell. However, towards the end of the year, a light broke in upon us.

Gabriel McLucre, the dean of guild's fifth son, a fine spirited laddie, somehow got suddenly a cadetcy to go to India; and there were uncharitably-minded persons who said that this was the payment for the Niggerbrae job to my lord.

JOHN GALT, *The Provost*, pp. 75–76 [Fiction]

1. How did the deacon of the masons in Edinburgh profit from his position?
2. Find the meaning of: dean of guild; factor; cadetcy?
3. Supply a suitable alternative for 'jookerie-cookerie'.

Choosing a Delegate

Delegates to choose a Member of Parliament for each group of burghs have already been mentioned in 'Scottish Representation in the British Parliament. To have influence in electing M.P.'s was often the main reason why landowners took an interest in burgh affairs:

I must say I prefer our own quiet canny, Scotch way at Irvine of electing a member of Parliament. Well do I remember that the Town Council, Lord Eglinton being then Provost, took in the late Thomas Bowet to be a councillor; and Thomas, not being versed in election matters, yet minding to please his lordship (for, like the rest of the Council, he had always a proper veneration for those in power) he consulted Joseph Boyd, the weaver who was then dean of guild, as to the way of voting. Joseph, who was a discreet man, said to him, 'Ye'll just say as I'll say, and I'll say what Bailie Shaw says, for he will do what my lord bids him,' which was as peaceful a way of sending up a member of Parliament as could well be devised.

JOHN GALT, *The Ayrshire Legatees*, p. 154 [Fiction]

1. How did Thomas Bowet become a councillor?
2. Who decided how the council should vote in this matter?

To guide your writing.
1. Why would the members of the councils of Edinburgh or Nairn or Ayr believe that they were best fitted to manage the town's affairs then?
2. Write an essay on: A criticism of Scottish town councils before 1833.

11 · SCOTLAND AND THE FRENCH REVOLUTION

Scottish Opinions about Events in France

In 1789 the States-General, the French parliament, met for the first time for a hundred and seventy-five years, and proceeded to reform abuses in the country and establish parliamentary government as in Britain. By capturing the Bastille prison on 14th July the Paris mob played their part and soon the Declaration of the Rights of Man proclaimed that all power belonged to the people. It seemed to be the dawn of a new age of freedom and dignity for men everywhere. Much foreign opinion, especially at first, was sympathetic to the French people in their struggle.

ENTHUSIASM: Andrew Fletcher was an Edinburgh lawyer who campaigned for the reform of town councils and Parliament:

At this time, 1791 and 1792, the grand principles of the French Revolution occupied the thoughts and stirred the passions of all thinking and feeling men. Mr. Fletcher was an ardent admirer of the first principles of that revolution. He loved liberty, not out of party spirit, but because he firmly believed that a free government was the only means of promoting national improvement and happiness. I believe he would have gone to the block in defence of his principles as cheerfully as any martyr that ever bled in that good cause.

ELIZABETH FLETCHER, *Autobiography*, pp. 64–65, ed. by LADY RICHARDSON, 1876

In his poem, 'A man's a man for a' that,' Robert Burns proclaimed his faith in the brotherhood of man, one of the ideals cherished also by the revolutionaries in France. Burns tried to help the French in a practical way by sending them four carronades but the guns were not allowed to leave Britain:

> Then let us pray that come it may
> As come it will for a' that,
> That sense and worth, o'er a' the earth,
> May *bear the gree*, and a' that;   [surely triumph
> For a' that, and a' that,
> It's coming yet for a' that,
> That man to man, the world o'er,
> Shall brithers be for a' that!

124

OPPOSITION: A former M.P. and an agricultural improver, George Dempster in old age expressed his feelings in a letter to Sir Adam Fergusson in Sept. 1792:

The horrors of this French Revolution sicken me at the human race and have corrected a great deal of my democratical spirit. I pray for the King, the House of Lords and its bench of bishops and band of Scotch peers every morning.

Letters to Sir Adam Fergusson, p. 222

In *A Scotch Antique*, Miss I. W. Brodie recalled her fears as a young child at the time of the Revolution:

I remember the thrill of horror which in 1793 pervaded society on receipt of the intelligence of the death of Louis XVI, and that I retired to rest that evening in the firm conviction that the French would be in Edinburgh in the morning.

INDIFFERENCE: The newspapers, then were all in a blaze of the bloody revolution in France – Robespierre, Danton, Carnot; the guillotine and the 'Tree of Liberty'; Pitt, Fox, the trials of Muir and others; Liberty, Slavery, Reform, Revolution.

I could comprehend none of these matters and my father seemed to take no notice of them.

JOHN YOUNGER, Shoemaker, *Autobiography*, pp. 40–41

1. What principles of the French Revolution were admired by (*a*) Archibald Fletcher and (*b*) Robert Burns?
2. Why were George Dempster and Miss Brodie opposed to the French Revolution?

To guide your writing:

1. Read an account of the French Revolution and try to explain why a poet like Burns should favour it and a former M.P. like Dempster oppose it.
2. Find out all you can about the personalities named by John Younger.
3. Sum up in your own words and explain the different attitudes of Scottish people to what was happening in France.

The French Revolution and the Reform Movement at Home

As events in France became more violent by 1792, with the King deposed and a republic proclaimed, the Tory Government under the Younger Pitt, and even some members of the Whig opposition, began to fear that a similar revolution might break out in Britain.

To some people outside Parliament, however, such as the members of the United Societies of Paisley France was an inspiration which fired them to campaign for wider representation of the people in the House of Commons in Britain. Pitt, who had previously tried without success to pass a bill for this very purpose, now turned his face against all reform. Although the reformers resolved 'to obey and respect the laws of their country' and Lord Cockburn maintained that there were very few real revolutionaries in Scotland, the trial of Thomas Muir proved that the Government would not tolerate any measure of reform at this time. To be a reformer was to be suspected of being a revolutionary:

THE POLITICAL PARTIES AND REFORM: The news of events in France and the knowledge of disloyalty at home, in those troubled days, was rapidly destroying all due balance between the political parties of Britain. On the one side was the ever-increasing multitude of terror-stricken Tories, toasting King George and the glorious Constitution, and passionately denying the unspeakable corruption and bad government of their country. On the other, was the resolute but rapidly diminishing band of Whigs, as vehemently denouncing the evils of their day, but under their breath, for the fear of Botany Bay was upon them. And meanwhile, all over the land, both in England and in Scotland, a great third party was rising, into whose hands power might at any moment fall – an undisciplined, discontented rabble, crack-brained and fanatical, wielding the most dangerous of all weapons, the demand for the right thing at the wrong time. French Revolution or no French Revolution, this party clamoured for instant Reform.

> KATHERINE STEUART, *Richard Kennoway and His Friends*, p. 53 [Fiction]

1. (*a*) What were the attitudes of the Tory and Whig parties to reform?
   (*b*) Why was the number of Whigs diminishing?
2. What is meant by: the glorious Constitution; corruption; the fear of Botany Bay?
3. (*a*) What was 'the right thing' the third party was struggling for?
   (*b*) Why does the writer think this was 'the wrong time'?

REPUBLICANS AND REFORMERS: We had wonderfully few proper Jacobins; that is, persons who seriously wished to introduce a republic into this country on the French precedent. There were plenty of people who were *called* Jacobins, because this soon became the common nickname which was given, not only to those who had admired the dawn of the French liberation, but to those who were known to have any taste for any internal reform of their own.

> LORD COCKBURN, *Memorials of His Time*, pp. 73-74

1. What did (*a*) proper Jacobins and (*b*) people *called* Jacobins want, according to Lord Cockburn?
2. Which of these two phrases do you think applies better to 'the third party' in the previous extract, and why?
3. What do you think Lord Cockburn's own attitude was towards reform?

THE MOVEMENT FOR PARLIAMENTARY REFORM: In Scotland many branches of the Society of the Friends of the People were formed in the bigger towns. This example of Paisley is typical:

REFORM
PAISLEY, Nov. 2, 1792

At a meeting of Delegates chosen by the United Societies of Paisley, associated for Parliamentary Reform, held in the Saracen's Head Inn, the following Resolutions were agreed to:

(1) That the object of these United Societies is, by all lawful means, the attainment of an equal Representation of the People in Parliament.

(2) To act in conjunction with the Society of the Friends of the People in London, and all other Societies in Britain, constituted for the same laudable purposes.

(3) To obey and respect the laws of their country. But it is the right of Britons to point out grievances, and petition for redress. By persevering steadily in this manner we will gain our cause, and the esteem of all good citizens.

ARCHD. HASTIE, President
ROBT. REID, Vice-President
WILLIAM REID, Secretary.
Edinburgh Gazetteer, Nov. 16, 1792

1. (*a*) What was the aim of the United Societies?
   (*b*) By what means did they hope to achieve this aim?
2. Can you suggest why the Government might fear the formation of branches of the Society of the Friends of the People at this time?

THE TRIAL OF THOMAS MUIR: The driving force in the Society of the Friends of the People in Scotland was an eloquent young lawyer, Thomas Muir of Huntershill. He was active in recruiting members and making speeches in which he attacked the system of electing members of Parliament, who represented only town councillors and landowners. The Government considered him dangerous and he was arrested. At his trial in Edinburgh before Lord Braxfield he was found guilty on three charges: encouraging working people to read revolutionary books such as Tom Paine's *The Rights of Man*, reading an address from the United Irishmen at the Convention of the Friends of the People, and making speeches stirring the people against the Government.

Muir spoke at great length at his trial, but his attitude to reform may be summed up in a single sentence of his speech defending himself:

> My crime is having dared to be a strenuous and active advocate for an Equal Representation of the People in the House of the People.
>
> P. MACKENZIE, *Life of Thomas Muir*, p. 106, 1831

The judge, Lord Braxfield, made a classic and reactionary defence of the British system of government before Muir was found guilty and sentenced to fourteen years transportation:

> The British Constitution is the best that ever was since the creation of the world and it is not possible to make it better. For is not every man secure? Does not every man reap the fruits of his own industry and sit safely under his own fig-tree?
>
> What right has such a rabble to representation? In this country the Government is made up of the landed interest which alone has a right to be represented. As for the rabble, who have nothing but personal property, what security has the nation for the payment of their taxes. They may pack up all their property on their backs and leave the country in the twinkling of an eye, but landed property can not be removed.
>
> P. MACKENZIE, *Life of Thomas Muir*, pp. 107–8, 1831

1. (*a*) On what charges was Thomas Muir found guilty?
   (*b*) Which of these do you think would be considered to be most serious at that time and why?
2. In Lord Braxfield's opinion, why was the British Constitution the best in history?
3. (*a*) Who alone, according to Lord Braxfield, should be represented in Parliament and why?
   (*b*) Why did he believe 'the rabble' should not be represented?

To guide your writing.

1. Explain why at that particular time (*a*) the Society of the Friends of the People gained so much support for their campaign for Parliamentary reform and (*b*) the Government was so fearful of reform.
2. Write speeches for (*a*) the prosecution and (*b*) the defence at the trial of Thomas Muir.

12·SCOTSMEN AND THE WAR AGAINST FRANCE, 1793–1815

The Armed Forces and the Danger of Invasion

Britain declared war against the French Republic in 1793 and British citizens, many of whom had previously sympathised with the ideals of the French Revolution, found their native country in danger of invasion by the French.

Recruiting for the Army

Some men, like Robert Flockhart and Alexander Alexander, answered the recruiting sergeant's call and joined the regular army:

I enlisted with a recruiting party for a regular regiment in the year 1797, about the time the soldier's pay was advanced from sixpence to a shilling. I was never flogged all the time I was in the army and that is what very few of the young soldiers could say. It was no uncommon thing to see ten or twelve men flogged before breakfast.

ROBERT FLOCKHART, Autobiography, p. 45

'As your friend, I give you my advice,' said the sergeant of the Royal Artillery. 'Enlist at once, my brave young fellow; if you enlist now you will receive this day's pay, and you may think yourself very fortunate to get into so fine a corps. It is the best and most honourable under the Crown. We have superior pay, superior clothing, little marching, always riding with the guns when on expedition.'

He assured me that I would be a sergeant in six months and an officer in a year or two at the very farthest. I agreed to join. He at once laid down a shilling which I took up, as an earnest that I was willing to serve my king and country in his Majesty's 6th Battalion of Royal Artillery. After drinking his Majesty's health and success to his arms, I went cheerfully to David Dale, Esq., Charlotte St. and was attested (25th April, 1801). This ceremony was to me a very serious thing, as it was done with due solemnity; I looked upon it as a very binding obligation.

The bounty I received was eight guineas, five guineas at present and the other three, intended for regimental necessaries, as soon as I joined the regiment.

Life of Alexander Alexander, by himself, 1830

The first Seaforth Highlanders enlisted in 1778 during the War of American Independence and a second battalion was raised just after the declaration of war against France in 1793 by Francis Humberston Mac-Kenzie of Seaforth. Within four months the battalion was at full strength and after being inspected at Fort George became the 78th Regiment of Foot. It is typical of the many Highland regiments recruited at this time:

The Corps is to consist of one Company of Grenadiers, one of Light Infantry and eight Battalion Companies.

No man is to be enlisted above thirty, or under five feet five inches; but well-made growing lads between sixteen and eighteen years of age, may be taken at five feet four inches.

The recruits are to be engaged without limitation as to the period or place of their service; but they are not to be drafted into any other Regiments; and whenever a reduction is to take place, they shall be marched into their own country in a Corps and be disembodied there.

Letter of Service to FRANCIS HUMBERSTON MACKENZIE OF SEAFORTH, 7th Mar. 1793, quoted by JOHN SYM in Seaforth Highlanders, pp. 12–13

1. (a) How much per day was the ordinary soldier paid about the year 1800?
   (b) What was the significance of Alexander Alexander 'taking up the shilling'?
   (c) How much did Alexander Alexander receive as a bounty and why do you think it was paid to him?
2. Why did the sergeant speak to Alexander Alexander as he did?
3. (a) Who was David Dale? (See The Coming of Cotton).
   (b) What was the ceremony of attestation which took place in his presence?
4. (a) Who raised the second battalion of Seaforth Highlanders and gave it its name?
   (b) What age did recruits have to be and how tall?
   (c) Is it true to say Seaforth Highlanders were required to serve anywhere and for as long as the Government pleased?

Recruiting for the Navy

The defence of Britain's shores was the Royal Navy's chief responsibility but as the Navy expanded in wartime, it was always difficult to recruit enough sailors. At this time about half of the crew of every fighting ship consisted of 'pressed' men, who were taken either from the crews of merchant ships at sea or from seamen in the ports.

This passage from Landsman Hay (pp. 216–20), the Memoirs of a Scottish seaman called Robert Hay, describes how he was 'pressed' into service. 'Landsman' was a fairly new rank in the Navy, lower than 'Ordinary Seaman' to describe men not yet skilled in their duties:

London 1811.

In a moment I was in the hands of six or eight ruffians who I immediately dreaded and soon found to be a press gang. They dragged me hurriedly along through several streets . . . into the presence of the Lieutenant of the gang, who questioned me as to my profession. I therefore acknowledged that I had been a voyage to the West Indies and had come home carpenter of a ship.

I was ushered into the presence of the examining officer and he thus addressed me:

'Well, young man, I understand you are a carpenter by trade.'

'Yes, sir.'

'And you have been at sea?'

'One voyage, sir.'

'Are you willing to join the King's Service?'

'No, sir.'

'Why?'

'Because I get much better wages in the merchant service and should I be unable to agree with the Captain I am at Liberty to leave him at the end of the voyage.'

'As to wages,' said he, 'the chance of prize money is quite an equivalent . . . Take my advice, my lad, and enter the service cheerfully. If you continue to refuse, remember you are aboard (cogent reasoning), you will be kept as a pressed man and treated accordingly.'

I refused. He said no more, but making a motion with his hands I was seized by two marines, hurried along towards the main hatchway with these words thundered in my ears, 'A pressed man to go below.' I was thrust down among five or six score of miserable beings, who, like myself had been kidnapped.

1. Where was Hay when he was arrested?
2. Why was he unwilling to join the Royal Navy?
3. What was 'prize money'?
4. If Hay was a skilled carpenter, why do you think he was given only the rank of 'Landsman'?
5. How many 'pressed' men did he find below?

The Danger of Invasion

Many men became part-time soldiers in the Volunteers and trained to help to defend the country:

Burns at once enrolled himself in the bands of gentlemen volunteers of

Dumfries, though not without opposition from some of the haughty Tories, who had doubts about his principles which they called democratic. I remember well the appearance of that respectable corps: white breeches and waistcoat, short blue coat faced with red; and round hat, surmounted by a bearskin, like the helmets of our horse guards; and I remember the Poet also – his very swarthy face, his very ploughman-stoop, his large dark eyes and indifferent dexterity in the handling of arms. At this time he wrote:

> Does haughty Gaul invasion threat
> Then let the louns beware, sir
> There's wooden walls upon our seas
> And volunteers on shore, sir . . .
> Be Britain still to Britain true
> Among oursels united
> For never but by British hands
> Maun British wrangs be righted!
>
> The wretch that would a tyrant own
> And the wretch, his true-sworn brother
> Who would set the mob above the throne
> May they be damned together!
> Who will not sing, *God save the King*
> Shall hang as high's the steeple;
> But while we sing *God save the King*,
> We'll ne'er forget the people!

This song hit the taste and suited the feelings of the humbler classes; hills echoed with it: it was heard in every street, and did more to right the minds of the people than all the speeches of Pitt and Dundas or of the chosen 'Five and forty'.

ALLAN CUNNINGHAM, *Life of Burns*, vol. 1, pp. 117–18

1. (*a*) Why did some of the Tory Volunteers in Dumfries think that Robert Burns should not have been allowed to join them?
   (*b*) What evidence have you already found to support their view?
2. Did Burns look a smart soldier?
3. Explain the meaning of: democratic; Gaul; wooden walls; volunteers; the chosen 'Five and forty'.

Peace dawned in 1802 and the French invaders had not come. But when France, now under Napoleon, declared war in the following year the danger to Britain seemed more serious than ever. The enlistment of Volunteers and their military preparations have been described by many writers. In *Annals of the Parish*, p. 145, John Galt recorded the excitement among the weavers of Ayrshire while Elizabeth Grant in *Memoirs of a*

Highland Lady, pp. 66–68, praised the patriotism of the farmers of Rothiemurchus. The extracts given below concern Edinburgh and the Borders, where French troops were at any moment expected, and in one case, the signal was given that they had indeed landed:

There is now little else talked of than the French invasion and everyone seems to think they will attempt to land at Leith very shortly from Holland. I have heard much of the same subject all summer but never took alarm till now; however, I must say I feel extremely anxious about it particularly on account of my Husband and Brother, who I fear will be called out to fight against these hell-hounds . . . but GOD Almighty in His infinite Goodness will, I hope, protect us all.

4th Nov., 1803, *Journal of Jessy Allan*, ed. W. PARK,
Book of the Old Edinburgh Club, vol. 30, p. 94

After the war broke out again in 1803, Edinburgh, like every other place, became a camp, and continued so till the peace in 1814. We were all soldiers, one way or another.

Walter Scott's zeal in the cause was very curious. He was the soul of the Edinburgh troop of Midlothian Yeomanry Cavalry. It was not a duty with him, or a necessity, or a pastime, but an absolute passion. He drilled, and drank, and made songs, with a hearty conscientious earnestness which inspired or shamed everybody within the attraction. I do not know if it was usual, but his troop used to practise, individually, with the sabre at a turnip, which was stuck on the top of a staff, to represent a Frenchman, in front of the line. In his turn, Walter pricked forward gallantly, saying to himself, 'Cut them down, the villains, cut them down!' and made his blow, which from his lameness was often an awkward one.

LORD COCKBURN, *Memorials of His Time*, pp. 117–18

In 1803 the threatened invasion of Bonaparte caused extensive measures to be adopted. A general volunteer force was raised all over Britain. This I joined, not so much out of any felt loyalty but to save myself in the event of my being drafted as a regular militiaman for the French wars all over the world.

Our drilling was then carried on by two or three neighbouring parishes meeting weekly on some central field, where we would march, countermarch, attack, charge, retreat, retire, and defend the day long and then be summoned to headquarters in Kelso for a fortnight or three weeks general drill in the 'fall'. Beacons were erected on all the hills around to give the signal should the French force get out of harbour, escape our fleet, or attempt to effect a landing.

On 31st January 1804, about ten at night I saw a red meteor-like light in the distance, which might be a beacon light. Up blazed Penielheugh, and Hume Castle with all the other signal hills on flame. Here was the signal, summoning every man to his musket. We had not yet got regimental red coats, and so we marched as we were, in our various coloured raggery. We of the village were soon collected, ready, and off ten miles to Kelso.

By one in the morning we were all in to answer roll call from all the country around. Just two individuals out of five hundred were a-missing. It being resolved to dismiss us to billets, Adam and I found ourselves very snugly feather-bedded in Mr. Swan's, Horse Market.

When out we got to morning parade, no satisfactory answer could be given why, how, where, or wherefore, these beacons were kindled all over the south of Scotland.

JOHN YOUNGER, Shoemaker *Autobiography*, pp. 221–9
Caverton Edge

Marcus Gunn, sergeant of the party stationed at the signal post here . . . said that about half-past nine o'clock on the night of Tuesday, the thirty-first day of January last he saw a light at Hume Castle which, appearing not very distinct he waited about twelve minutes; and the light [at Hume Castle] still continuing to burn he immediately hoisted his signal. He declared that about four minutes before he hoisted his own signal he saw the light at the Dunion and immediately after, Penielheugh took up the signal, and then Crumhaughhill. About half an hour after Hume Castle was lighted he saw Duns Law burn very bright and about the same time.

Adv. M.S. 31.1.23 National Library of Scotland 1804, *Evidence of Marcus Gunn*

1. Where did Jessy Allan think the French would land?
2. (*a*) What feelings moved Sir Walter Scott to join the Midlothian Yeomanry Cavalry?
   (*b*) What was John Younger's main reason for joining the Volunteers?
3. (*a*) How were people in the south of Scotland to be warned if the French were about to land?
   (*b*) What happened there on the night of 31st January 1804?
   (*c*) What did John Younger's company do that night?
   (*d*) Why did Marcus Gunn light his beacon?

To guide your writing.
1. Using the information in the extracts, write accounts of: (*a*) recruiting for the regular army and the navy and (*b*) the raising and training of the Volunteers.
2. Describe the spirit of the people during the invasion scares, and illustrate your answer by reference to the extracts.
3. Write a description of 'The False Alarm' (1804).

Kirkman Finlay and the Continental System

Kirkman Finlay, son of the founder of James Finlay and Company, merchants in Glasgow, acquired cotton mills, such as Catrine in Ayrshire, and expanded trade with Europe, India and America. He later became Lord Provost of Glasgow and M.P. for Glasgow:

The Napoleonic Wars made trading with the Continent increasingly difficult and the normal obstacles of war developed into a complete prohibition when the Berlin Decrees, which were meant to kill British trade with the Continent, were issued [in 1806]. Napoleon's military power was supreme and he was able to enforce his will on all the subject nations. To the British merchants, the future appeared to hold very poor trading prospects. It was as if a wholesale merchant suddenly found that a rival had stationed armed men at the doors of all his best customers to bar the sale of his goods.

No challenge could have stimulated Kirkman Finlay more effectively. He intended to defy the blockade and carry on his trade notwithstanding Napoleon's decrees and no one in Britain succeeded better or on a larger scale. A favourable factor was the resentment of the Continental nations and their willingness to collaborate in any scheme to defeat the blockade. There was no possibility of supplanting British goods from elsewhere and the shutting out of British sources of supply caused great hardship in Europe as well as at home.

In 1807 [he] established a House (John Thomson and Company) in the island of Heligoland as a depot to supply the North of Germany and in 1809 established one in the isle of Malta from which to supply the South. Cotton yarn for Austria and Switzerland was sent from Malta to Salonica and then by a long land journey to Vienna, a great part of the way on the backs of horses.

Kirkman Finlay's Evidence (*Parliamentary Papers,* 1812) to a Parliamentary Committee enquiring into the state of trade and employment:

'Are you interested in any very considerable manufactory in or near Glasgow?'

'Yes, in the spinning and manufacture of cotton; it employs from about two to three thousand people.'

'Are you also a merchant extensively concerned in commerce in Glasgow?'

'Yes.'

'Have you considerable correspondence in different parts of Europe and other parts of the world?'

'At the commencement of the war in 1803, the number of correspondents, of the trading house in which I am engaged, on the continent of Europe, was about 700.'

'In what state have the manufactures of Glasgow and its neighbourhood been in the course of the last eighteen months?'

'In a state of considerable depression. The trade was at its worst probably, about the months of May and June, 1811, but it has gradually, and very slowly begun to improve. The condition of the people was very bad, and their wages were low. Low wages were forcing a great number of persons out of employ.'

James Finlay and Company, 1750–1950, pp. 14–15, 17–18, 20–21

1. Why was trade with the Continent more difficult in wartime?
2. What was the intention of Napoleon when he issued the Berlin Decrees?
3. Why did Napoleon think he would succeed?
4. What was the attitude of Continental peoples to the Berlin Decrees and why?
5. Why did the blockade cause great hardship (*a*) in Europe (*b*) at home?
6. What two islands became Finlay's bases for breaking the blockade?
7. What other business interest did Finlay have besides trading?

To guide your writing.

1. Find out from a historical atlas which countries were dominated by Napoleon in 1806?
2. (*a*) What was the main commodity which Finlay exported to Europe?
   (*b*) Make a map to show its route from Glasgow to Vienna.
3. Imagine you were a British exporter who traded with the Continent at this time. In a letter to a client in Danzig, explain your difficulties and propose a plan to deliver an order to him.
4. Do you think the British Government approved or disapproved of Finlay's activities and why?

MODERN MODERATION STRIKINGLY DISPLAYED

Dismiss; I order every one of you, go home and desire your Parents to teach you I have a right to be heard I say go Home —

Sir some of them have no Parents

OR

A MINISTERIAL *VISITATION* of a SABBATH EVENING SCHOOL.

PLATE 24. The Rev. W. Moody disperses a Sunday School – such meetings were frowned on by the Moderate clergy.

PLATE 25. Edinburgh Royal Volunteers. (See pp. 131–3.)

13·DISCONTENT AFTER 1815

Causes of Discontent

The Corn Law

The Corn Law of 1815 prevented wheat from abroad being imported into Britain until the home price reached 80s a quarter. This practically gave full freedom in the home market to British farmers to sell their grain at high prices and to landowners to continue to charge high rents for farms. For the poor, dear grain meant dear food:

Glasgow
11th March, 1815.

The minds of the people are much occupied in speculating about this Corn Bill. You will no doubt have heard of the partial riot which we had here on Tuesday last and that they broke a few panes of glass to Kirkman Finlay. The same spirit still continues and is manifested by the great number of effigies which have been hanged and the picture which they put up. Yesterday about 3 o'clock poor Finlay was represented hanging upon a gibbet upon one of the pillars of the Tontine. This instantly collected a great multitude who testified their joy by huzzahs and laughter. After some time the picture was taken down by a police officer and taken to the office. The same disposition prevails in Gorbals, Tradeston, Anderston, Calton and Bridgeton and if the Bill is passed serious consequences may be expected.

Letter of MATTHEW ALLISON, quoted in
James Finlay and Company, pp. 27–28

Were it not for these restraints [the Corn Law 1815], we might be able to purchase the same quantity of bread for 40s or at most 50s, that now costs 70s or 80s. The interest of the farmers in the question of the corn laws is exactly the same with that of the consumers. If prices were permanently reduced, rents would fall in proportion, bad land would be thrown out of cultivation and the profits of agriculture would rise. By permitting the free importation of foreign corn no real injury would be done to the landlords; for assuredly they have no right to be benefited at the expense of the other classes. It is the duty of Government to facilitate the investment of the capital and industry of the country in those departments in which it will yield the largest returns; not certainly to give undue advantages to any one class at the expense of the rest.

The Scotsman, 6th May, 1820

1. How did people in Glasgow react to the attempt to pass the Corn Bill and why?
2. Who was Kirkman Finlay?
3. If the Corn Law were repealed, according to *The Scotsman* article, (*a*) how would consumers benefit? (*b*) how would farmers benefit?

Unemployment

In the years after 1815, the number of unemployed rose because of a slump in trade and the return of discharged soldiers and sailors:

> Edinburgh
> May 1818

Dear John,
These three months I can find nothing to do. I am a burden on Jeanie and her husband. I wish I was a soldier again. I cannot even get labouring work. I would be useful but can get nothing to do. I will go to South America or I will go to Spain.

Journal of a Soldier in the 71st Regiment, H.L.I.

> Selkirk
> 9th May, 1817

I am glad to see you are turning your mind to the state of the poor, for I have kept about thirty of the labourers in my neighbourhood in constant employment this winter. This I do not call charity, because they executed some extensive plantations and other works, which I could never have got done so cheaply, and which I always intended one day to do. But neither was it altogether selfish on my part, because I was putting myself to inconvenience in incurring the expense of several years at once, and certainly would not have done so but to serve mine honest neighbours.

Sir Walter Scott, Letter to Robert Southey, from *Letters of Sir Walter Scott*, ed. by GRIERSON, vol. 4, p. 446

1. What did the soldier think he would do?
2. Why did Sir Walter Scott employ the thirty labourers?

Distress among Handloom Weavers

The plight of the weavers after 1815 was hard to bear compared with their earlier prosperity, which had resulted from their skill and a plentiful supply of machine-spun yarn:

In 1797 these weavers in Anderston (near Glasgow) were a class apart. Many of them, skilful workers, could earn as much as nearly four shillings for each yard of muslin that left their looms. They had money in plenty to buy food, and unlike the ill-nourished workmen of the eighteenth century, they were so stalwart and well-grown that the recruiting sergeants had their eye upon them and would fain have tempted them to enter his Majesty's service. But the weavers preferred the cheerful clickety-clack of their own handlooms to the roar of Boney's cannons or to the groans of dying men on a field of battle. Their tastes were intellectual, not war-like; they could afford to buy books, and most of them read, or studied as they worked; whilst on the Saturday half-holiday, in an age of con-stant toil already claimed as a right by the weavers, they met together and discussed with the greatest intelligence the affairs of Church and State or keenly debated some difficult question of philosophy or political economy.

KATHERINE STEUART, *Richard Kennoway and His Friends*, p. 171 [Fiction]

HAND-LOOM WEAVERS IN GLASGOW, 1814–1819:

	1814 per day		1815 per day		1816 per day		1817 per day		1818 per day		1819 per day	
Average wage, based on 12 hour day and 6 day week.	s	d	s	d	s	d	s	d	s	d	s	d
	2	2¾	1	11½	1	2¼	0	11¼	1	2¾	0	10¼

Prices	1814		1815		1816		1817		1818		1819	
	s	d	s	d	s	d	s	d	s	d	s	d
Oatmeal per peck	1	9	1	6	1	6	1	10	1	10½	1	3
Potatoes per peck	0	11	0	10	1	3	1	5	1	0	0	10
Good beef per lb.	0	9	0	8	0	7½	0	8½	0	8	0	7½
Coarse beef per lb.	0	7	0	6	0	5	0	6	0	6	0	5½
Bread (fine) per quartern loaf	1	0	0	10½	1	2½	1	4½	1	2	0	11¾
Bread (coarse) per quartern loaf	0	9	0	7½	0	9	0	11¾	0	10	0	8¾
Fresh butter per lb.	1	4	1	4	1	4¾	1	6	1	4	1	1
Coals per 12 cwt.	7	0	7	3	7	0	6	3	5	6	5	6
House rent of two apartments	100	0	100	0	100	0	100	0	95	0	90	0

Report of James Cleland, Superintendent of Public Works, for H.M. Government, printed in *The Scotsman*, 13th May, 1820

1. In what ways were the weavers 'a class apart'?
2. How did their standard of living compare with other workmen at the end of the eighteenth century? (See Standards of Living, Life in the Country.)
3. What right did they claim, which other workers had not yet achieved?

4. (a) What is the general trend of wages between 1814 and 1819?
   (b) Which years are extreme examples of this trend?
   (c) Roughly, how do wages in 1819 compare with 1814?
5. If for the poor, the cost of living is the cost of the cheapest foods, e.g. potatoes, oatmeal or coarse bread, study the prices of these articles, compare them with the wages in the upper table and decide which was (i) the year of greatest plenty and (ii) the year of greatest hardship.
6. (a) What is the trend in prices between 1814 and 1819 and is it more or less extreme than the trend in wages?
   (b) What conclusions have you reached about the condition of the weavers by 1819?

To guide your writing.
1. Contrast the circumstances of the weavers in 1817 with their position twenty years earlier.
2. Summarise the causes of discontent between 1815 and 1820, which led to 'the Radical War' (see below).
3. Explain why conditions after 1815 were worse in industrial towns than in the country districts.

'The Radical War', 1820

Were the workers in Glasgow and its neighbourhood about to embark on armed revolution in 1820 or did the authorities magnify the threat in order to use military force to intimidate a few determined workers? That is the problem posed by 'the Radical War'. The Glasgow magistrates and the editor of the *Glasgow Courier*, a loyal and conservative newspaper, expressed their alarm. Lord Cockburn, a Whig lawyer in Edinburgh, however, writing after the event and knowing that the few marchers had been easily dealt with, ridiculed the Government's fears and elaborate precautions:

300 POUNDS REWARD
WHEREAS, certain Wicked, Evil-disposed and Traitorous Persons, during the night of the 1st, or on the morning of the 2nd, of April instant, did FELONIOUSLY, TRAITOROUSLY and DARINGLY in furtherance of a CONSPIRACY to compass or imagine the Death of Our Lord the King, or to LEVY WAR AGAINST OUR LORD THE KING, within his Realm, or to commit other Treasons, PUBLISH and AFFIX on the walls and public places in many parts of the City and Suburbs of Glasgow and other parts of the County of Lanark, a most WICKED, REVOLUTIONARY and TREASONABLE ADDRESS to the Inhabitants of Great Britain and Ireland, dated at Glasgow, April 1

1820 and bearing to be issued 'by order of the Committee of Organisation
for forming a Provisional Government', directly and openly PRO-
CLAIMING REBELLION AGAINST OUR LORD THE KING AND
THE LAWS AND CONSTITUTION OF THE REALM, inciting and
stimulating the subjects of Our Lord the King to take up Arms for the
overthrow of the Government and Constitution, as by Law established,
and TO LEVY WAR AGAINST OUR LORD THE KING, The LORD
PROVOST and MAGISTRATES of the City of Glasgow, SHERIFF
of the County of Lanark and JUSTICES of the PEACE for the Lower
Ward of Lanarkshire, hereby offer a

REWARD OF

THREE HUNDRED POUNDS

to any Person or Persons who shall, within fourteen days from this date,
DISCOVER and APPREHEND, or cause to be DISCOVERED and
APPREHENDED, those guilty of THIS OVERT ACT OF HIGH
TREASON, by printing, publishing and issuing the said Revolutionary
and Treasonable Address, under the said Treasonable designation of
the Committee of Organisation for forming a Provisional Government.
Glasgow, 4th April, 1820

Notice in the Glasgow Courier, April 1820

1. Use a dictionary to find the meaning of any words you do not
   understand in this notice.
2. Judging from the wording of the document, what did the magis-
   strates fear would happen in Glasgow and Lanarkshire?
3. What was the actual offence complained of?

April 3.

All the weavers in Glasgow and its suburbs have struck work, and our
streets are crowded with them walking about idle. The weavers in
Paisley have also ceased to work and it is not improbable that we may
be favoured with a visit from some of them. The colliers in the country
round about have likewise struck this morning.

About mid-day the Dunbartonshire Yeomanry Cavalry arrived in
town and in the afternoon the Ayrshire Yeomanry Cavalry. More troops
are expected in the course of the day. Several troops of the 10th Hussars
and the 80th Regiment of Foot marched from Edinburgh yesterday
morning for this district.

In some places strangers have taken possession of smiths' shops, who
instantly fell to work making pikes, etc.

The times are perilous in the extreme.

April 4.

Between 30 and 40 Radicals armed with guns, pistols, pikes, etc., apparently from Glasgow, marched through the village of Cordorrat, about ten miles east from this city, in military order. They took two guns from people in the village.

April 6. ALARMING STATE OF THE COUNTRY

It is out of our power to express our present perilous situation. Hourly and momentarily, night and day, alarms are given.

ENGAGEMENT WITH THE RADICALS
FROM AUTHORITY

Yesterday morning, 5th April, two men of the Stirlingshire Yeomanry returned to Kilsyth and reported the presence of a party of armed Radicals a few miles away. Lieutenant Hodgson of the 10th Hussars, and Lieutenant Davidson of the Stirlingshire Yeomanry, immediately marched with a party of each of those corps in pursuit of the men, whom they overtook near Bonnybridge. On observing this force, the Radicals cheered and advanced to a wall, over which they commenced firing at the military. Some shots were then fired by the soldiers in return, and, after some time, the cavalry got through an opening in the wall and attacked the party who resisted till overpowered by the troops, who succeeded in taking nineteen of them prisoners. In this encounter, Lieutenant Hodgson received a pike-wound through the right hand and a sergeant of the 10th Hussars was severely wounded by a shot in the side and by a pike. Three horses were also wounded. Four of the Radicals were wounded, one of whom was left on the field, 5 muskets, 2 pistols, 18 pikes and around 100 rounds of ball cartridge were taken.

Twelve o'clock – All is quiet here at present.

Glasgow Courier

1. (*a*) What kind of workers were involved?
   (*b*) What is a 'Radical'?
   (*c*) What preparation did the Radicals make?
2. Do you think that on 3rd April the authorities considered they had enough troops to deal with the situation?
3. How serious did the *Glasgow Courier* think the situation was?

The year 1819 closed, and the new one opened, amidst the popular disturbance called 'The Radical War'. The whole island was suffering from great agricultural and industrial distress. But it was first exaggerated, and then exhibited as evidence of a revolutionary spirit, which nothing but Toryism and Castlereagh could check. It was determined therefore that the folly and violence of our western weavers should be considered as a civil war, and be dealt with accordingly. Edinburgh was as quiet as the grave, or even as Peebles.

The Mid-Lothian Yeomanry Cavalry was marched, in the middle of a

winter night, to Glasgow; remained in the district a few days; did nothing, having nothing to do; and returned, as proud and as praised, as if
fresh from Waterloo.

Some people, however, were clear that a great blow would be struck
by the Radical army – by an army, much talked of but never seen. Our
magistrates therefore invited all loyal citizens to congregate, with such
arms as they had, at various assigned posts. I repaired to the Assembly
Rooms in George Street, with a stick, about eight in the evening. On
entering the large room, I found at least 400 or 500 gentlemen pacing
about, dressed coarsely, as if for work, and armed with bludgeons, fowl-
ing pieces, dirks, cane swords, or other implements. At last, about ten
p.m. the horn of the coach from Glasgow was heard, and the Lord Provost sent us word that we might retire for the night. We never met again.

LORD COCKBURN, *Memorials of His Time*, p. 212

1. What causes does Cockburn suggest for 'the Radical War'?
2. What comments does he make on the parts played by the Yeomanry Cavalry, and the loyal citizens in Edinburgh?
3. Why was it safe for the citizens to go home at 10 p.m.?

To guide your writing.

1. Bearing in mind (*a*) the actions of the workers, reported in the
   Glasgow Courier on 3rd and 4th April and (*b*) the number of
   casualties and the number of weapons captured, how dangerous
   did this event turn out to be?
2. Do you think it deserves to be called 'the Radical War'?

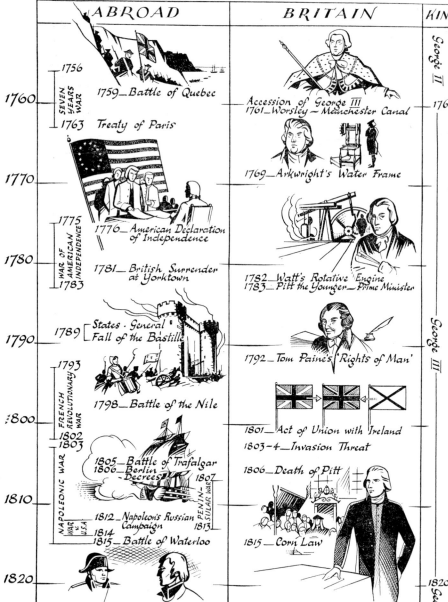

ABROAD

BRITAIN

George II

1756

1760

SEVEN YEARS WAR

1759—Battle of Quebec

1763 Treaty of Paris

Accession of George III
1761—Worsley — Manchester Canal

1760

1770

1769—Arkwright's Water Frame

1775

WAR OF AMERICAN INDEPENDENCE

1776—American Declaration
of Independence

1780

1781—British Surrender
at Yorktown

1783

1782—Watt's Rotative Engine
1783—Pitt the Younger—Prime Minister

1789

States · General
Fall of the Bastille

1790

1792—Tom Paine's 'Rights of Man'

1793

FRENCH REVOLUTIONARY WAR

1798—Battle of the Nile

George III

1800

1802
1803

1801—Act of Union with Ireland

1803–4—Invasion Threat

NAPOLEONIC WAR

1805—Battle of Trafalgar
1806—Berlin
Decrees

1807

PENINSULAR WAR

1806—Death of Pitt

1810

WAR v. U.S.A.

1812—Napoleon's Russian
Campaign

1813

1814
1815—Battle of Waterloo

1815—Corn Law

1820

1820

George IV

SCOTLAND

POLITICAL	ECONOMIC & SOCIAL	LITERATURE & THE ARTS

LITERATURE & THE ARTS

1755 — Dr. Webster's Census
1756 — John Home's Play, 'Douglas' in Edinburgh

1760 — Perth Academy

1773 — Dr. Johnson to the Hebrides

1776 — Adam Smith's 'Wealth of Nations'

1783 — GLASGOW ADVERTISER (later HERALD)

1786 — Robert Burns' Kilmarnock Edition

1791 — (Old) Statistical Account's First Volume

1802 — EDINBURGH REVIEW
1803 — Education Act

1814 — Walter Scott's 'Waverley'

1817 — SCOTSMAN BLACKWOOD'S MAGAZINE

WAVERLEY NOVELS

ECONOMIC & SOCIAL

1759 — Carron Iron Works

1769 — Patent for Watt's Steam Engine

1778 — First Cotton Mill at Penicuik

1786 — New Lanark
1788 — First Steamship
1790 — Forth & Clyde Canal

1799 — End of Serfdom for Colliers

1802 — Symington's CHARLOTTE
1803 —   DUNDAS

1812 — Bell's COMET

1819 — Sutherland Clearance (Strathnaver)
1822 — Caledonian Canal

TELFORD IN HIGHLANDS

POLITICAL

1782 — Repeal of Laws against Highlanders
1784 — Forfeited Estates Restored

1793 — Trial of Thomas Muir

1801

1804 — 'The False Alarm'

REFORM

1820 — 'Radical War'
1822 — George IV's visit to Edinburgh

14·THE INCREASE IN POPULATION, 1755–1821

COUNTY	Webster 1755	1801	1821	% increase 1801–21
1. Aberdeen	116,168	121,065	155,049	28
2. Angus	68,883	99,053	113,355	14
3. Argyll	66,286	81,277	97,316	20
4. Ayr	59,009	84,207	127,299	51
5. Banff	38,478	37,216	43,663	17
6. Berwick	23,987	30,206	33,385	10
7. Bute	7,125	11,791	13,797	17
8. Caithness	22,215	22,609	29,181	29
9. Clackmannan	9,003	10,858	13,263	22
10. Dumfries	39,788	54,597	70,878	30
11. Dunbarton	13,857	20,710	27,317	32
12. East Lothian	29,709	29,986	35,127	17
13. Fife	81,570	93,743	114,556	22
14. Inverness	59,563	72,672	89,961	24
15. Kincardine	23,057	26,349	29,118	10
16. Kinross	4,889	6,725	7,762	15
17. Kirkcudbright	21,205	29,211	38,903	33
18. Lanark	81,726	147,692	244,387	65
19. Midlothian	90,412	122,597	191,514	56
20. Moray	30,604	27,760	31,398	13
21. Nairn	5,694	8,322	9,268	11
22. Orkney	23,381	24,445	26,979	11
23. Peebles	8,908	8,735	10,046	15
24. Perth	120,116	125,583	138,247	10
25. Renfrew	26,645	78,501	112,175	43
26. Ross and Cromarty	48,084	56,318	68,762	22
27. Roxburgh	34,704	33,721	40,892	21
28. Selkirk	4,021	5,388	6,637	23
29. Stirling	37,014	50,825	65,376	29
30. Sutherland	20,774	23,117	23,840	3
31. West Lothian	16,829	17,844	22,685	27
32. Wigtown	16,466	22,918	33,240	45
33. Zetland	15,210	22,379	26,145	17
TOTAL	1,265,380	1,608,420	2,091,521	30

J. G. KYD, *Scottish Population Statistics.*

These census figures are provided for you to refer to and to use. A census is an exact check on the number of people in a country on a particular date and the first official census was taken in 1801. Since then

a census has normally been repeated every ten years. The figures showing
the population of the counties of Scotland in 1755 were collected by Dr.
Webster, the minister of the Tolbooth Church of Edinburgh, with the
help of parish ministers. They are considered to be very reliable and
Scotland is fortunate in having the results of a survey made at such an
early date.

1. Find the total increase in population (*a*) between 1755 and 1801,
   (*b*) between 1801 and 1821.
2. Do the same for your own county.

As the figures show, this was a time of population growth. The percentage increase between 1801 and 1821 for the whole of Scotland was
30 per cent and every single county showed an increase, some large, some
small. The greatest was in Lanarkshire, which showed an increase of 65
per cent, while Sutherland, with only 3 per cent, had the lowest percentage increase.

Many causes have been suggested for the rise in population at this
time. It seems to have been due partly to a decline in the death-rate:
people were living longer, because of the increased quantity and improved
quality and variety of foodstuffs, and advances in hygiene and medical
care. Contributing also to population growth was a rise in the birth-rate,
at this time of great economic change when the demand for labour
brought higher wages, earlier marriage and more births.

While the overall increase may be explained by the reasons given above,
the variation between counties can only be accounted for by local conditions, which caused people to migrate from one area to another. Where
the percentage increase was low, it may have been caused by:

(*a*) the amalgamation of farms (see *New Statistical Account* for the
     county) when small tenants were dispossessed;
(*b*) the introduction of sheep-farming which required less labour;
(*c*) clearance and emigration;
(*d*) the attraction of neighbouring towns.

Increases above average may have been due to:

(*a*) agricultural improvements, which increased the demand for village
     craftsmen, foresters, gardeners, labourers, etc.
(*b*) the development of the fishing industry.
(*c*) new industries, e.g. cotton attracting workers from elsewhere, like
     the many Highlanders employed by David Dale at New Lanark.

1. Try to find the reasons for changes in population in your county
   being above or below the national average.
2. Try to do the same for any other county you know well.
   The appropriate volume of the *New Statistical Account* will be
   helpful.

FOR FURTHER STUDY

The sources of the extracts used in this book will have suggested a great deal for further reading but four books written by people living at the time are particularly recommended:

Memoirs of a Highland Lady, a delightful record of her life on Speyside in the heart of the Highlands by Elizabeth Grant of Rothiemurchus, the daughter of a landowner, lawyer and Member of Parliament.

The Autobiography of John Younger, Shoemaker, for life in the Borders.

Annals of the Parish by John Galt, a work of fiction which relates realistically the events in the life of a minister in an Ayrshire parish.

Memorials of His Time by Lord Cockburn, a rich collection of portraits of famous people and stories of life in Edinburgh from 1779–1830, with lively comments on education, religion and politics.

OTHER ASPECTS:

    Local History: The two Statistical Accounts

    Poetry: The Poems of Robert Burns

    Paintings by: Allan Ramsay, David Allan, Henry Raeburn and David Wilkie. See *Forty Scottish Paintings*, published by the National Galleries of Scotland or, better still, look for their works in art galleries

    Architecture: The New Town of Edinburgh by James Craig and others; Register House, Edinburgh and Culzean Castle, Ayrshire by Robert Adam. See *A History of Architecture in Scotland* by T. W. West (University of London) and *The Age of Adam* by J. Lees-Milne (Batsford)

    Costume: *Scottish Costume* by S. Maxwell and R. Hutchinson (A. & C. Black)

    Food: *The Scots Kitchen* by F. Marian McNeill (Blackie)

    Music: *The Scots Song Book* (4 vols) by H. Wiseman and J. Eason (Nelson)

COLLECTIONS OF DOCUMENTS:

Scottish Diaries and Memoirs 1746–1843, edited by J. G. Fyfe (Eneas Mackay), a scarce book but a valuable collection of long extracts

Source Book of Scottish Economic and Social History, 1707 to the present, edited by R. H. Campbell and J. B. A. Dow (Blackwell), fairly long extracts

Scottish Pageant, vol. IV, 1707–1802, edited by A. M. Mackenzie (Oliver and Boyd), short passages arranged for pleasure.

MODERN GENERAL WORKS:

Economic History of Scotland in the Eighteenth Century, by N. Hamilton (O.U.P.)

The Social Life of Scotland in the Eighteenth Century, by H. Grey Graham (Black)

The Domestic Life of Scotland in the Eighteenth Century by M. Plant (Edinburgh University Press)

Highland Folk Ways by I. F. Grant (Routledge)

SUBJECT INDEX

Burns, Robert, 85, 100, 124, 131

Canals, 56
  Highland, 72
Carpets, 25, 26
Carron Iron Works, 28
Carronades, 29
Caschrom, 60
Cattle trade, 13, 16
  Trysts, 13–14, 15
Church of Scotland, 92
  secessions, 92–3, 95
Clearances, in Sutherland, 77
Continental System, 135
Corn Law, 137
Cotton Trade, 21
  effects of, 22
Culloden, consequences, 2–3

Dale, David, 130
Drovers, 14
Dundas, Henry (Lord Melville), 116
Dyeing, of cotton, 22
  of wool, 25, 26

East India Co., 119
Edinburgh, 81
  commerce of, 84
  Town Council, 121
Enclosure of common land, 9
  benefits from, 11
  sufferings caused by, 10
Erskine, Ebenezer, 92

False Alarm, The, 133–4
Farming, before improvement, 6
  Highland, 60
  improvements in, 8
  rise of values from, 12
Finlay, Kirkman, 135, 137
Fishing, from Stornaway, 2
Fodder, winter shortage, 7
Forfeited estates, 65
French Revolution, 124

Glasgow, 87

Highlands, travel in, 69
Highland regiments, 67
Highlanders, life of, 59
  changes in, 64
Houses, Highland, 61
Hume, David, 85

Industry, wages in, 41–3
Iron industry, 28, 30
  charcoal in, 28

Jacobins, 126

Linen trade, 18

Mackenzie, Henry, 85
Moderates and Evangelicals, 94–6
Muir, Thomas, trial of, 126, 127

New Lanark, 21

Old Statistical Account of Scotland,
  12

Parchment barons, 12
Parliamentary reform movement, 127
Parliamentary representation, 112
Patronage Act, 93
Peat, 63
Pension list, 116
Ploughs, 7
  James Small's, 9
Poor, maintenance of, 96–7
Press gang, 131

Radical War, 140
Recruitment, army, 129–30, 132–3
  navy, 130
Roads, Highlands, 69–71
  Lowlands, 49
Robertson, Dr. William, 85
Rotation of crops, 9
Runrig possession, 6

Sabbath, observance, 98–9, 103

INDEX OF SOURCES

ACKNOWLEDGEMENTS

The author and publishers are grateful to the following for permission to reprint copyright material: Cambridge University Press for the extracts from *James Watt* by H. W. Dickinson; Carron Company for the extracts from *Carron Company* by R. H. Campbell; The Clarendon Press, Oxford, for the extracts from *Economic History of Scotland in the Eighteenth Century* by H. Hamilton; Constable & Co. Ltd, for the extracts from *Henry Dundas, First Viscount Melville* by Cyril Matheson; Sir James Fergusson of Kilkerran, Bt., for the extracts from *Letters of George Dempster to Sir Adam Fergusson* edited by Sir James Fergusson; James Finlay & Co. Ltd, for the extract from *James Finlay & Co*; Rupert Hart-Davis Ltd, for the extract from *Landsman Hay* by M. D. Hay; Hollis & Carter Ltd, for the extract from *Stage Coach to John o'Groats* by Leslie Gardiner; Lutterworth Press for the extract from *The Drover Lad* by Kathleen Fidler; Eneas Mackay Publications, for the extract from *Prophecies of the Brahan Seer* by A. Mackenzie; Thomas Nelson & Sons Ltd, for the extract from *The Dawn of Scottish Social Welfare* by T. Ferguson; Oxford University Press, for the extract from *Henry Dundas, 1st Viscount Melville* by H. Furber; Selwyn & Blount (Hutchinson & Co. (Publishers) Ltd), for the extracts from *Scottish Canals and Waterways* by E. A. Pratt.

The author and publishers are grateful to the following for permission to reproduce the illustrations as follows: Sir Ilay Campbell Bt., for *Highland Dance*, Plate 6; Carron Company, Falkirk, for the print of Falkirk, Plate 2; Edinburgh Corporation Libraries and Museums Department, for the illustrations used in Plates 11, 12, 13 and cover; I. Donnachie, for the photograph of New Lanark, Plate 3; T. Hunter, for the John Kay portraits, Plates 8, 14, 17 and 24; Inverness Town Council for the painting of *Thomas Telford*, Plate 10; The National Coal Board, Lothians Division, for colliery plan, Plate 4; The Board of Trustees, The National Galleries of Scotland, for the paintings reproduced in Plates 5, 7, 15, 16, 18, 20, 21, 22 and 23; The Trustees of the National Library of Scotland, for the newspaper reproductions on Plate 19; The B.B.C. and the Scottish Record Office, for the East Lothian Estate Plan, Plate 1.